MOSES AND ME

Moses and Me

A Journey through the Book of Exodus

Jean M. Schultz

CROSSBOOKS
PUBLISHING

CrossBooks™
A Division of LifeWay
1663 Liberty Drive
Bloomington, IN 47403
www.crossbooks.com
Phone: 1-866-879-0502

Scriptures taken from the Holy Bible, New International Version®,
NIV®. Copyright © 1973, 1978, 1984, 2011 by Biblica, Inc.™ Used by
permission of Zondervan. All rights reserved worldwide. www.zondervan.
com The "NIV" and "New International Version" are trademarks registered
in the United States Patent and Trademark Office by Biblica, Inc.™

First published by CrossBooks 08/21/2013

ISBN: 978-1-4627-3070-4 (sc)
ISBN: 978-1-4627-3071-1 (e)

Library of Congress Control Number: 2013913838

Printed in the United States of America.

This book is printed on acid-free paper.

Any people depicted in stock imagery provided by Thinkstock are models,
and such images are being used for illustrative purposes only.

Certain stock imagery © Thinkstock.

CONTENTS

Introduction

In the beginning, God created the world and everything in it. He created man to have a relationship with Him. In the book of Genesis, we see God in all His glory create a perfect place for the first man and woman. Throughout the Bible, we learn the history of mankind, and we bear witness to God's sovereignty and power as He draws His chosen people to Himself. It is a history that describes the fall of man and the treachery of the human heart and how God desires to draw His chosen people to a life of fellowship with Him.

As you get ready to join Moses and me, it is important that you understand the circumstances of God's people and the events that led to their painful captivity in Egypt. The following "key" verses from the book of Genesis will help you understand how the book of Exodus is the continuation of God's relationship with His chosen people, the Hebrews (referred to as the Israelites throughout this story). Exodus is also the story of God's spectacular rescue mission to bring them back to the land He promised to Abraham, Isaac, and Jacob through the faith and empowerment of His chosen deliverer, a man named Moses. All scripture references throughout the book are from the New International Version of the Bible.

God Creates the World

In the beginning God created the heavens and the earth.

Genesis 1:1

Adam and Eve

So God created man in his image, in the image of God he created him; male and female he created them.

Genesis 1:27

The Fall

So the Lord God banished
him from the Garden of Eden
to work the ground from
which he had been taken.

Genesis 3:23

God Sends the Flood

The Lord said to Noah, "Go into the ark, you and your whole family, because I have found you righteous in this generation."

Genesis 7:1

God Begins again with Noah's Family

Then God blessed Noah and his sons, saying to them, "Be fruitful and increase in number and fill the earth."

Genesis 9:1

Abraham Receives God's Blessings

He took him outside and said, "Look up into the heavens and count the stars—if indeed you can count them." Then he said to him, "So shall your offspring be."

Genesis 15:5

Isaac Is Born

Then God said, "Yes, but your wife Sarah will bear you a son, and you will call him Isaac. I will establish my covenant with him as an everlasting covenant for his descendants after him."

Genesis 17:19

The Lord Speaks to Isaac

"I am with you and will watch over you wherever you go, and I will bring you back to this land. I will not leave you until I have done what I have promised to do."

Genesis 28:15

Jacob Steals Esau's Birthright

But he said, "Your brother came deceitfully and took your blessing."

Genesis 27:35

Joseph Is Jacob's Favorite Son

Now Israel loved Joseph more than any of his other sons, because he had been born to him in his old age; and he made a richly ornamented robe for him. When his brothers saw that their father loved him more than any of them, they hated him and could not speak a kind word to him.

Genesis 37:3-4

Joseph Is Sold to the Ishmaelites

Judah said to his brothers, "What will we gain if we kill our brother and cover up his blood? Come, let's sell him to the Ishmaelites and not lay a hand on him; after all, he is our brother, our own flesh and blood."

Genesis 37:26

✝

Innocent Joseph Is Imprisoned

But while Joseph was there
in prison, the Lord was with
him; he showed him kindness,
and granted him favor in the
eyes of the prison warden.

Genesis 39:20-21

Joseph Interprets Pharaoh's Dreams

Then Joseph said to Pharaoh,
"The dreams of Pharaoh are one
and the same. God has revealed to
Pharaoh what he is about to do.
Seven years of great abundance
are coming throughout the
land of Egypt, but seven years
of famine will follow them."

Genesis 41:28-29

Joseph Reconciles with His Brothers

"I am your brother, Joseph, the one that you sold into Egypt. And now, do not be distressed and do not be angry with yourselves for selling me here, because it was to save lives that God sent me ahead of you."

Genesis 45:4-5

Joseph's Final Instructions

Then Joseph said to his brothers, "I am about to die. But God will surely come to your aid and take you up out of this land to the land he promised on oath to Abraham, Isaac, and Jacob."

Genesis 50:24

CHAPTER 1

MURDER AND RUN
EXODUS 1-2:15

Moses: Greetings. I am Moses, a servant of the living God, and my story is mostly about Him and how He delivered His people, the Hebrews—also known as the nation of Israel—following four hundred years of slavery. God had a mighty purpose in giving me life. He has a great purpose in giving you life, and it is the hope of my heart that you see His hand and feel His Spirit through the retelling of my story.

I was born in Egypt. My parents were Amram and Jocabed, Hebrew slaves. My brother, Aaron, and my sister, Miriam, were older than me. It was a perilous time to be alive. The Hebrew people had grown from a family of seventy to a nation of millions. We lived in the land of Goshen, in northeast Egypt. We were enslaved to build the pharaoh a mighty and expansive empire; it was the most architecturally advanced civilization the world had ever seen. As the pharaoh surveyed his land, he was pleased with the magnitude of his kingdom. The weekly progress

1

of construction was impressive. However, the pharaoh feared our numbers and envisioned an uprising that made him nervous, so he gave an order to the Hebrew midwives that they kill any infant boys born to Hebrew women. He said that the Egyptian soldiers would observe the women and would severely punish them if they did not comply with his order.

The midwives prayed to God for guidance and empowerment; they feared God more than they feared Pharaoh, and many male babies survived. They explained to the soldiers that the Hebrew women had delivered their children quickly. The midwives couldn't get to the women in time, and that prevented them from complying with Pharaoh's order.

The midwives were not the only ones who had been given an order to murder innocent life. Pharaoh's soldiers went from house to house, looking for anyone they suspected of hiding a baby. Many babies were thrown into the Nile, but my parents hid me from the soldiers—and God kept me safe.

The time arrived when my mother knew she could no longer keep me quiet. She had an inspired idea. She made a basket boat for me, wrapped me in a blanket, placed me in the sacred vessel, and took me to the shore of the Nile. Prayerfully, my mother put me in the water. She knew God would protect me and provide me with a new home where I would be safe. My mother sent Miriam to watch where I drifted so she could report when I was drawn out of the water by someone who would care for me. My mother's prayers were answered.

Pharaoh's daughter was bathing in the river when one of her servants spotted my woven boat floating among the reeds. She retrieved the basket and carried me to the princess. As she lifted my blanket, I started to cry. She knew I was the baby of a Hebrew slave.

Miriam, who had been watching, approached them and asked if they needed a wet nurse for me. The princess said yes, and Miriam returned with my mother, Jocabed. The princess offered to pay my mother to nurse me until I was weaned.

My infancy and early childhood were full of joyful moments with my precious family. My parents instilled in me an awareness of my true heritage. I heard the stories of previous generations and how God had blessed them. My family also told me of a promise from the Lord. God would send a deliverer to rescue His people and return them to the land from which they had come. My mother and my sister were musically gifted, and I learned the love language of God as they sang each day. I embraced the importance of expressing faith and honoring the Lord through music and worship. Once I was weaned, I was returned to the princess and was raised as her son.

My childhood was privileged. I lived in the palace of the pharaoh, the ruler of Egypt, the greatest nation in the world. My education was extensive. I learned how to read and write. I learned about science and culture. Being close to the pharaoh, I learned many lessons about leadership and self-discipline.

Once I was an adult, I watched the Hebrews building the pharaoh's kingdom and empathized with their painful captivity. I ached for the women and children who labored relentlessly. The men were overworked and downtrodden. One day, when I was walking through the streets, I witnessed an Egyptian soldier beating a helpless slave mercilessly. The soldier whipped him repeatedly until the slave was lying on the ground, bloody and unable to stand. My soul was ignited with an overwhelming empathy. I grabbed the soldier's arm, threw him to the ground, and inflicted the same harsh punishment on him. I didn't stop until the soldier was dead. I looked around, hoping my deed had been unobserved. I buried the man in the ground.

What I had done was criminal. The pharaoh would have punished me severely if he had found out. Out of guilt and shame, I started to run. I left the land of Egypt, not wanting to be put to death for murder. Before I left, I sought the appreciation of the Hebrew community. I hoped they would look to me as their deliverer, but I did not find that confirmation in their expressive faces; they knew my actions would only increase their suffering and labor.

As I reflect now, I realize that in that moment I had stopped being an Egyptian prince and had returned to being a Hebrew slave. Would the pharaoh forgive me? Because of the Hebrews' passivity, I was afraid to find out, so I ran. I knew what I was running from, but I had no idea where I was going. I needed to escape from Egypt, from the pharaoh, and from the Hebrews, who didn't embrace me as their deliverer.

I could not run from myself, however. The guilt, shame, and disappointment in my soul were all-consuming. This painful remorse had the potential to destroy me. I knew I had to escape to a new land where no one knew who I was or what I had done.

Jean: Hello. My name is Jean. It is the hope of my heart that in sharing my story with you, you will come to know that my God and Moses' God are the same. I am an ordinary, middle-aged woman. What could have happened to me that remotely parallels Moses' life? I will attempt to answer that in this book. My prayer for you is that you will be moved to faith and will know that God still uses people to advance His kingdom. Moses and I will proclaim His truth, tell of His sovereign love, and reveal His plan for those who worship and follow Him.

My mother was an "inconvenient" child, being the youngest of seven. She was an innocent victim in the exhausting life of her mother. My grandmother was weak and weary from the demands of her family. She was frustrated with my grandfather and ultimately divorced him. She walked away from her family when my mother was only eleven. My grandmother moved to an apartment in her hometown that was too small to keep her children with her. Because of my grandmother's selfishness and the fact that my grandfather was deemed unfit to care for his children, my mother and my uncle were sent to a children's home.

Over time, my mother became a rebellious, angry teenager. She got into so much trouble that she was sent to a juvenile detention center. She continued her self-destructive patterns of behavior and at age fifteen was consequently sent to a state prison for women.

My mother was allowed to visit her family for a weekend once or twice a year. During one of those trips, she became pregnant with me. She was told that the handsome man she had been introduced to was an unmarried fellow who thought she was pretty. She returned to prison hoping that he would be waiting for her when she was to be released the following year. She later learned in a letter from her sister that she had been lied to; he was a married man with children. My mother was devastated. The prison personnel began to wonder if she was pregnant, and this was confirmed when she saw a doctor in her fifth month. She was sixteen when I was conceived.

My mother wrote to her oldest sister, asking if she would keep me until she was released from prison. I was supposed to be born in April, and she wasn't going to be released until the following December. My aunt agreed to take me. Three weeks before my birth, however, my mother received a letter from her sister explaining that she couldn't add another baby to her already large family. My mother was deeply saddened and acutely distressed about what would happen to me.

I was born in April 1960—right on schedule—in a hospital in Fond du Lac, Wisconsin. I was removed from the delivery room as soon as I was born; my mother was not allowed to see me until the next day. She was permitted to gaze at me through the nursery glass as I slept in a bassinet. The prison and hospital officials had her sign documents placing me in foster care. She did not sign anything that gave up her parental rights. She returned to the prison with a heavy heart and empty arms. She resumed her routine of duties and healed physically and emotionally from her pregnancy.

Since my mother was legally a minor, her father was given the authority to make decisions for her (her mother had died four years before my birth). He gave the doctors consent to sterilize his daughter after my birth. He went to court to terminate her parental rights so I could be adopted. He did not communicate any of these decisions to my mother; she did not find out about them until she was released from prison at age eighteen.

Once released from prison, she married a man who had been one of the guards at the prison and moved to Chicago. (There will be more details about this relationship later in the story.) She appealed the validity of the documents regarding the termination of her parental rights but lost her legal fight to be reunited with me. I was legally adopted by my foster family on May 3, 1962, at age two.

The upper-middle-class family that adopted me settled in a small but growing town in southern Wisconsin. My parents were medical professionals. I was the second oldest of their five children and the only one who had been adopted. My childhood was turbulent at times, but mostly it was safe and good.

My father was very strict; he emphasized educational success as a condition of his approval. He had little tolerance for mediocrity or "average" intelligence, which was my nature to a fault. I put forth solely the minimum effort in my schoolwork and spent most of my time concentrating on my social life. My father and I had our conflicts, and I turned to relationships with boys and sought out their approval and acceptance. In my teens, I experimented with sex and drugs and always had a boyfriend to spend time with. I gave those boys control when it came to our physical relations, and my self-esteem suffered because most of the time I allowed them to take advantage of me.

My first full-fledged sexual encounter would probably (by today's standards) be considered date rape. It happened three days after my sixteenth birthday. It was a time of acute instability for me emotionally, and my low self-worth rationalized the way I was being treated. I continued to make self-destructive choices that were detrimental to my health and well-being.

Nonetheless, I managed to graduate from high school and started college. I moved out of my parents' house when I was eighteen and lived in a nearby town as I attended college.

My high school sweetheart and I had been dating since the end of our junior year of high school. We found acceptance and approval within our relationship, something we had both struggled to find during our upbringing.

I was in the middle of my second year of college when the unthinkable happened—I got pregnant. I couldn't let my father know because I thought he would kill me! I confided in those who were close to me at that time and was told I had only one choice, abortion. The picture of the life they were telling me I would lead if I didn't have an abortion was difficult to hear. I couldn't risk the probability of being cut off from those I loved, so I had no choice but to agonizingly submit to their will. There would be no marriage or happily ever after, which is what I was hoping for at that time.

My spiritual upbringing was Christian. I went through confirmation class and chose to be baptized into the faith at age fifteen. I was active in my youth group, and I had a basic knowledge of God and His Book. I believed with my whole heart that abortion was murder. My inner thoughts screamed at me but not loudly enough to trump my fears of being rejected by those I loved.

My boyfriend came to my apartment the night before the procedure. He watched a movie in my living room while I sobbed in the bathroom behind a closed door. He knew I was in a lot of emotional and spiritual pain, but he could not bring himself to have mercy and compassion in his words or actions that would have eased my suffering. He quietly knocked on the bathroom door, told me he was leaving, and asked me to call him the next day to tell him how it had gone. No one in his family ever learned what he had asked of me. I cried the remainder of the night and somehow fell into a restless sleep, praying that morning would somehow not arrive.

I went to the abortion clinic the next morning with my child clinging to my womb. For those of you who are unfamiliar with the practice and the procedures of abortion, a counselor first evaluates your mental and emotional well-being and assesses your ability to live with the decision of abortion. She had me talked out of it within a very short time; she reported to the doctor that I would suffer from remorse and that my recovery would be extremely traumatic. However, I told the counselor and the doctor I didn't have any other choice.

9

I followed through with the procedure I can still envision in my mind some thirty years later. The ever-present, consuming emptiness was at times unbearable in the weeks, months, and years following that dreadful day. My boyfriend was supposed to come to my apartment following the procedure to take care of me, but when I called his home, I was told he had gone fishing and would not be home until much later in the afternoon.

He had gone fishing! I had just undergone the ultimate expression of my love and devotion (he had told me our relationship would be over if I had the baby), but he did not choose to comfort or care for me in my greatest hour of need.

Because of my shattered soul, I ran from God. I was overwhelmed with guilt, shame, and remorse that spiritually paralyzed me. I considered myself unworthy of grace, mercy, or forgiveness. I wasn't worthy to call myself a Christian or a child of God Most High. I thought I was doomed to spend my life in a spiritual chasm of self-loathing and hopelessness.

I ran from God to create a distance from Him, hoping He wouldn't find me. It would be ten years before I would stand before Him again, broken and spiritually hemorrhaging. He was, however, preparing me to return to Him from a place of total desperation and despair. He confronted my denial of His lordship over me, and I reached the point of humility that He required, surrendered to His outstretched arms, and received His Spirit of transformational healing.

CHAPTER 2

REDEMPTION AND REST
EXODUS 2:16-25

Moses: Murder. The shame and guilt follows you wherever you go. I knew in my heart I could not return to my former families. For most of my life, my identity had been split in two. I struggled with balancing the life of privilege with the knowledge of having been born into a Hebrew family, having been spared only because of the actions of a sympathetic princess and her servant. I reflected on the events of my life and came to realize my former opinion of being some kind of savior for the Hebrews had been the result of an overactive imagination. God had not chosen to use me to save His nation. I had to reformulate my plan and seek a new path. I began walking east, through the desert, waiting for the opportunity to start fresh. I anticipated finding a new place and new people who would welcome an educated man and embrace him as a new member of their tribe or nation.

I came upon a well where people were having a dispute about water that had been drawn by two girls.

The girls were being harassed by travelers, and the girls were struggling to keep the water they had drawn from the well. I did not see any of their people nearby to defend them against these aggressive men. I stepped in and persuaded the men to leave them alone. The girls gathered their water and took me to meet their father; they wanted to tell him how I had helped them.

Their father, Jethro, embraced me and invited me to join their evening meal. I accepted the invitation and was honored for what some of them considered an act of heroism. I was drawn to this spiritual leader, Jethro, and his people. I was welcomed and offered a place among them. There was bountiful food, fellowship, and an ease in their honor and worship of God. I listened attentively and was drawn to him because he spoke of God's love and faithfulness with a spirit of conviction. I thought of my unworthiness; I thought of the murder I had committed and how I couldn't forgive myself. Jethro helped me to accept that our past transgressions make us into the humans we are and that God increases our faith throughout our difficulties. He also taught me that God uses our trials and mistakes to draw us to Him. Jethro spoke to my heart in the name of God. I repented, confessed my sin, and received undeserved favor from the Lord. Grace was offered to me, and I was forgiven.

In time, I fell in love with one of Jethro's daughters, Zipporah. She was beautiful, kind, and caring, and I asked her to be my wife. We married and settled down. In time, we welcomed two sons into our family. Life was simple. Life was good.

I embraced my roles as husband and father. I spent my time loving and instructing my children. It was simple living uncomplicated by my past, and I found inner peace. I was drawn into the life of the shepherd. I watched over the flocks and relished the days spent in the wilderness, where I had time to think, rest, and plan my family's future.

Many years passed. God used that time to draw me to Himself through prayer and meditation. I recalled many things about God my mother had taught me during my childhood. I talked to God, sometimes out loud, and other times just in my head. I thanked Him for the many blessings He had given me. I talked to my boys when they accompanied me to the pastures. At dinner each night, I offered my worship to God, who provided for our daily needs. I was truly content. I had uninterrupted rest in the fields as well as in the embrace of my family.

One of the most difficult aspects of my job as a shepherd was teaching the sheep that their safety and well-being were my responsibility. I was their protector. If they wandered too far, I had to retrieve them and return them to safety where I could watch over them. To help increase their awareness of my authority over them, I would break a leg of any sheep that wandered too far. After disabling it, I would carry the impaired lamb on my shoulders. While the animal would heal, its reliance on me would increase. Once the leg was healed, the lamb would return to being independently mobile, but it would never stray from me again.

I have found that God sometimes allows difficulties and hardships into our lives to draw us closer to Him.

He is my Shepherd. He wanted to train me not to stray from Him. Little did I know He was preparing to "break my legs" through a spectacular miracle and prompt me to return to Egypt, where I would confront the powerful pharaoh and command him to free the Hebrew nation from the bondage of slavery so they could live free and return to the land God had prepared for them.

Jean: As had Moses, I learned to live with the remorse and guilt of my choices from earlier in my life. I finished school and started working. I lived in a small town a few miles from my hometown and continued to date my high school sweetheart for many years. I had forgiven him for the past and tried to make plans for the future.

There were times, however, when I questioned whether he understood the degree to which I had sacrificed for him. It's hard to walk away from the level of commitment I demonstrated by my choice to kill our child. We didn't talk about it; I wanted him to love me. I couldn't walk away even though my hopes were unfulfilled and dimming. After eight years of dating, we decided it was either get married (which I wanted) or break up (which he wanted). We chose the latter.

At that time, I was working full time in a nursing home in southern Wisconsin near Lake Geneva and had a coworker who knew about my relationship status. She invited me to her house to meet a guy her boyfriend had gone to high school with. His name was Bob. It had been only three weeks since my former relationship had ended, but I went because I was tired of sitting around my apartment feeling sorry for myself.

I arrived at her apartment before he did, and we were sitting at the kitchen table when Bob came in. We were introduced, and I felt a connection with him right away. He was very sweet, very funny, and very conversational. He was kind and considerate as well.

After dinner, we went to a bar and played pool and darts. He followed me home to make sure I got there safely, and we made plans for the next day.

We got together several times over the next few weeks, and within the first month of dating, I knew in my heart he was the man I would eventually marry.

He had many friends, and we were socializing more than I had ever socialized before. It was a whirlwind romance, and we were engaged on the nine-month anniversary of our blind date. We planned a Valentine's Day wedding and spent the next eleven months anticipating and preparing for our life together.

We married on a cloudy February afternoon. The wedding was perfect, and the reception was amazing. We were picked up from the reception by a limo, and the driver took us to my parents' house so we could change our clothes and get our bags. The limo driver took us to a hotel near the airport where we spent our wedding night. Early the next morning, we caught a plane to Puerto Vallarta, Mexico, our honeymoon destination. It was all very romantic, and we were so thankful. Life could not have been any better. We were so blessed.

CHAPTER 3

LISTENING TO GOD'S VOICE
EXODUS 3-4:20

Moses: Close to my eightieth birthday, I was watching the sheep in the pasture. I noticed one of the lambs wander away over a small hill. I followed it and came upon a bush that was burning. I got closer and saw that while it was full of flames, its branches were not being consumed. I was very curious, and I was somewhat afraid when I suddenly heard a voice coming from within the fire itself: "Moses, Moses. Take off your sandals, for the ground you are standing on is holy ground."

I was startled and fell to the ground. I removed my sandals and stood, grabbing my staff. I was shaking with fear. I said, "Here I am."

God said, "I have surely seen the oppression of My people in Egypt, and I have heard their cry because of their taskmasters; I know their sorrows. So I have come to deliver them out of the hand of the Egyptians and to bring them to a good and large land, a land flowing with milk and honey. I have also seen the oppression with which the Egyptians oppress them. Come, therefore, and I will send you to Pharaoh that you may bring My people, the children of Israel, out of Egypt."

The God of the Israelites had just told me I needed to return to Egypt because He was going to use me to free them from the pharaoh! I wanted to tell him, "Been there, done that," and I tried my best to convince Him I was the wrong guy for the mission, but He told me my objections were not going to sway Him. I asked, "Who am I that I should bring the children of Israel out of Egypt? Suppose they will not believe or listen to my voice?" I protested further. "Oh my Lord, I am not eloquent . . . I am slow of speech and tongue." My final objection was, "O my Lord, please deliver them by someone other than me."

The Lord reassured me that He would be with me and that I could ask my brother, Aaron, to speak on my behalf. I continued my efforts to persuade Him to reconsider His commission, but it was His command that I do this work for Him. Resigned and overwhelmed, I accepted the mission.

I returned to my home and told my family about the burning bush and the voice that had commanded me to return to Egypt. I told them that I would be reunited with the family I had rejected by running away and that they would help me face Pharaoh. My wife and the rest of my family were surprised to hear of my encounter with God. They asked me to repeat the story several times, but in the end, they encouraged me to follow the Lord's instructions and leave the land we had called home for the past forty years.

I was a reluctant prophet, but I readied my family for the journey so I could honor God and His request. In my mind, I was fearful of being persecuted for having committed murder. In my mind, I was fearful the Hebrews would reject my leadership. In my mind, I feared the powerful pharaoh and wondered if he would remember me. However, in my mind, I was not returning to Egypt alone; my Lord would be with me. He would use me and His power to free His people. That knowledge was the source of my strength. I surrendered to His will. I fell to my knees and asked the Lord to forgive my self-doubt, fear, and reluctance. I repented and received His forgiveness.

Jean: The first year of our marriage was filled with joy, laughter, and celebration. We loved our families, friends, and coworkers. We had an active social life and enjoyed life to the fullest.

Shortly after our six-month anniversary, we found out I was pregnant with our first child. It was an exciting time. I felt a sense of reassurance that God had forgiven me for my past mistakes and that I was finally going to realize the dream of becoming a mother. Having been adopted, I had a place in my soul that yearned for a biological connection to others.

I anticipated the birth of my child with a sense of fulfillment because the baby would be the first person I would meet who shared my genes. I looked forward to seeing my baby for the first time; I envisioned finally looking into a face that represented my personal history.

My pregnancy was uncomplicated; I did not suffer from morning sickness or other common pregnancy maladies. My health remained good throughout each trimester. Bob and I prepared our hearts and our home to welcome the baby; we couldn't have been more content.

We were renting a townhouse in Racine, Wisconsin. We bought nursery furniture, had a baby shower at which we received many beautiful gifts, and waited for the birth. I resigned from my job so I could be a full-time mom.

My due date was May 1, 1988. Spring was a lovely time to celebrate new life. We went to bed that night wondering when I would go into labor.

I awoke at 1:30 a.m. and went to the bathroom. As I walked down the hallway, my water broke. I called our doctor, and he told us we should wait to go to the hospital in the morning because my labor pains had not yet started.

We talked to him again in the early morning, as I had not started having regular contractions. We went in to his office, and he checked to see if I had started to dilate, but I was just one centimeter. He told us to return home and get ready for an afternoon admission to the hospital. If I hadn't started regular contractions by then, he said, he would give me medication to get things rolling.

We got to the hospital as directed that afternoon. I checked in to a beautiful private room. We had decided not to notify our families until after the birth, so no one knew we were at the hospital.

I started labor in the early evening. We used the skills we had learned in childbirth classes, but by 9:00 p.m., I was ready for an epidural. That helped a lot, but

I was still dilating very slowly. The doctor talked about doing a C-section around midnight because it was close to twenty-four hours since my water had broken, but we declined since I was progressing.

At 3:30 a.m., I was fully dilated; I began pushing. Two hours later, our son was born. It was early morning on May 3, 1988.

The doctor had placed a fetal monitor to the baby's head and found he had a strong heartbeat throughout his delivery. That monitor was removed moments before he was fully out of the birth canal. I remember feeling him kick during the last few pushes but didn't think that was unusual. He was given to the nursing staff, and everyone became alarmed because he was very pale and not breathing—no pulse. We never heard him cry. The medical staff worked and worked on him; they did CPR, and they repeatedly tried to revive him. A neonatologist was brought in, and our son was taken to neonatal intensive care.

Forty minutes after his delivery, he was pronounced dead. Our doctor came in to our room and gave us the devastating news. We were numb.

Nothing in my life had caused such excruciating pain, even the time that followed my abortion. The doctor told us that when a baby dies, it is beneficial for the parents to see him, hold him, take some time to bond and come to grips with the cruel reality of such a tragic outcome.

When we were ready, the nursing staff brought us our baby boy. We held him, un-wrapped him, looked at his fingers and toes, and tried to memorize every detail of his tiny body. One of the nurses took pictures of us holding him and other pictures of him in the nursery. They made foot imprints on his birth paper they gave us. They also gave us a lock of his hair.

We were with our son for thirty minutes or so. I could not speak. My husband had the horrific task of calling our parents, extended family, and our close friends. I was moved to a room away from the maternity wing so I wouldn't have to listen to the babies and their mothers. I had a private room outside of which was posted a blue teardrop—a signal to the staff that we had lost a baby.

Our families lived an hour from the hospital, so it took a while for them to get there. Once they arrived, however, we were surrounded by love, comfort, and many teary eyes. Everyone was in a state of shock and devastation. I felt numb; I literally could not feel my body. I was unable to focus, listen, respond to questions, or process my thoughts about my new reality. I do remember telling my husband that God must think we were strong enough to handle this tragedy or wouldn't have allowed it to happen. My husband held me, and we grieved.

When evening arrived, Bob's best friends from high school were there to drive him to our apartment. They spent the night with him so he wouldn't be alone. A sympathetic nurse was my companion. She stayed with me and predicted that, providentially, I would return to the hospital in a year and a half or so and have a different outcome. She told me that I would go on to have other children and that God would bless our family. I listened and thanked her for her presence and encouraging words. I don't think she had to be there with me, but she provided grace and mercy for what I had been through and didn't want me to be alone. I don't remember her name, but I will never forget her kindness and compassion.

The next day, Bob's friends brought him back to the hospital early, and I was released. We were in agony as we drove through Racine to our home. We passed a school, and Bob had to pull over because he couldn't stop sobbing. Someone once told me that when you lose one of your parents, you lose your past. I feel that when you suffer the loss of a child, you lose your unfulfilled future.

We made it home. Of course, my body was aching for my infant. My arms yearned for my joyfully anticipated son, Austin. He was not with us, but we knew he was safe in the arms of the Lord.

The pastor who had married us arrived in the afternoon to help us plan a burial service. He prayed with us and sincerely expressed his sorrow and sadness. We asked our families to let people know we couldn't possibly deal with a large group, so only members of the immediate family were asked to attend the service. My sister-in-law bought me a dress for the funeral. The days between the birth and the funeral passed in a blur. I remember being terrified of being alone. I couldn't go into the nursery either, so we left its door closed; it was six weeks before we entered that room. I was in so much emotional agony that most of the time it felt I had to concentrate on every breath, and it was very hard for me to put words together. I was told I was in shock and would be for quite a while. All I knew was that I didn't want to be left alone.

On May 6, 1988, we buried our son. The autopsy was inconclusive as to the cause of his death. Our doctor later told us that he thought that there had been a break in the umbilical cord; our son's blood was being pumped into the placenta, but because of the break, it was not going back into his body. He had lost so much blood that the doctors' attempts to revive him were unsuccessful. I wondered if his kicking I had felt before the complete delivery could have caused the placenta to tear from the wall of my uterus. The cruel reality was that we would never know what had actually happened.

The day after the funeral, our closest friends came to our apartment to express their sympathy. We all cried and cried, and they offered as much encouragement as they could. We certainly appreciated their empathetic words and physical comfort.

My husband returned to the cemetery a couple times in the months following our son's death; it was five years, however, before I returned to Austin's grave.

Around Christmastime, my husband told me he had buried a toy soldier near our son's gravestone. I remember celebrating Christmas but feeling anxious for the end of the year. Cognitively separating ourselves from the worst year of our lives offered a reassurance that healing would come in the New Year and that hopefully, God would bless us again with new life.

We were told that 85 percent of marriages do not survive the death of a child. We were directed to a support group that could potentially make things easier for us to cope. We attended it a couple of times, but the people there had lost mostly older children. My husband and I turned to drugs and alcohol to deaden the suffering and pain. We would often drink and smoke pot until we passed out, a pattern we repeated for many weeks.

My journey with grief was a time of compromised communication—I couldn't translate my feelings into words. At this time of wanting release from my physical and psychological pain, I could not escape the thought that God had taken my son because I had had that abortion. Human logic and bad theology kicked in, and I told myself God and I were finally even. I had taken a life from Him, and He had taken a life from me.

Not everything in my life, however, was debilitating after the death of our son. I applied for a job about a month after his birth as the activity director at a Lutheran nursing home. I was responsible for all scheduled programming and oversaw a staff of seven. Because it was a Christian nursing home, a chapel service was broadcast throughout the building every day. The chaplain knew of my loss and was available to me for spiritual comfort. I thanked him for his thoughtfulness, but I didn't pursue his offer because at that time, facing God was so painful for me. I felt condemned, unworthy, rejected, and unable to stand before Him as a blameless sinner. However, even though I was outwardly denying my need for God, He was using the chaplain through his daily messages to speak truth to my soul and plant seeds of hope in my heart.

After choosing drugs and alcohol for a while, I pursued healing through secular therapy. I became the client of a woman who had a PhD in psychology and a thriving practice of helping people. She helped me very much in dealing with the remorse and regrets of my past choices and the guilt and shame I carried each day. She used a variety of methods to help me release the demons that had haunted my soul for many years. She helped me discover a new world in which I didn't have to be so hard on myself. She used hypnotism to look into my psychological past, and I received healing from many events and liberation from the guilt and shame of the abortion. She helped me psychologically learn the tools of meditation and relaxation.

However, there were spiritual issues I was unable and unwilling to face through my work with her. Ultimately, I realized that man-centered positions and thinking could not quench the fire in my soul that later I realized only God could put out and heal.

Ten months after the loss of our child, on the first day of spring, I discovered I was pregnant again. My due date was Thanksgiving Day. Talk about a sign from God! We had the hope and joy of new life and a grace that transformed into hope and healing, and we were sincerely grateful for our new baby. I felt a sense of freedom from fear and a revival of faith; I accepted that the outcome of this pregnancy would be in God's hands. I asked God for His blessing and protection as we once again hoped to welcome a new life into our family.

What would have been Austin's first birthday was a difficult day for us. We grieved with raw emotion that was softened somewhat by the new life growing inside my womb. That sad day was followed by days that were filled with hope for a fresh start.

Six months into this pregnancy, we bought our first house. We set up a nursery that was the same but different. We requested to have a C-section because we didn't want to go through labor and delivery again, and our doctor was very agreeable. We chose a day that was six days before Thanksgiving, the birthday of Bob's paternal grandmother. Because it was a scheduled procedure, our families and closest friends were at the hospital during the delivery. Our daughter was a healthy eight-and-a-half-pound gift from God. It was exactly a year and a half since we had lost our son, so the prediction given to me by the nurse on Austin's birth day had been realized and was snug in my arms.

In the next five years, we added two more daughters to our family. We relocated to a different state because of a job transfer, and I experienced for the first time a vibrant, thriving faith in Jesus Christ. The Lord sent women into my life who were mature in their faith and could help me nurture a personal relationship with Christ. They invited us to their church and their homes, and they encouraged me to a life of obedience and seeking. We found life-changing relationships in a community of faith.

One woman invited me to attend a women's Bible Study Fellowship (BSF) with her, an intense program that lasted thirty-two weeks. It emphasized structured study notes, group discussions, lectures, and gatherings. A teaching leader prepared lectures and oversaw the discussion leaders. There was also a great children's program. The lessons were divided into seven-day formats of study with notes and question-and-answer sessions. For the first time in my life, my faith was living and even active. I couldn't get enough of Bible study, and I recommitted my life to God. It was personal and life-altering. I had a new system of accountability that nourished my soul and transformed my mind.

After several years, I determined that the discipline of the program and the resulting personal growth were probably the most important spiritual gifts I had ever experienced. My husband often teased me that I attended more meetings each week than he did because I had become so active in our church.

As our family grew, I was so thankful to the Lord because each year when we remembered our son, Austin, on his birthday, I was either pregnant or nursing an infant. I believe it was God's way of comforting me and reassuring me that His compassion for me was greater than His condemnation of my past. Praise the Lord, for He is good.

Throughout that time of our life, when we were raising our children, we were not spared from challenges. I had a precancerous tumor removed from my thyroid, and I suffered a stroke due to birth control pills. Because of my tumor, I felt an urgency to find out about my medical family history. I petitioned the state of my birth, Wisconsin, for my closed adoption records. After six months of filling out and mailing in various forms, I received information about a part of my past in the mail. It was fascinating! I read and reread the documents. One of the most interesting parts of this history was the date when my adoption had been finalized was the same date we had lost our son, May 3rd! I experienced an emotional kinship with my birth mother because of this information.

Many parts of the records were blacked out because of confidentiality concerns, but I learned about my birth mother's childhood, her imprisonment, her pregnancy, my delivery, my earliest experiences as a foster child, and the details of my adoption.

The most shocking information for me was that she had been in prison when she was pregnant with me. I called my parents, and they told me they had known about that and that they were saddened I had found out. They wanted me to be spared from the knowledge so I wouldn't be emotionally hurt thinking she had been a criminal.

The most touching of the records was a letter my adoptive father had written, requesting that they be considered to legally adopt me. I was about eighteen months old when he wrote it. There were descriptions of my health and temperament as a toddler, and my husband thought it was very entertaining, because some of my early characteristics were evident in me as an adult.

I was frightened by many details about my birth family, however. I read that my birth mother had many emotional problems and some violent tendencies. I found out some members of her family were criminals.

The second part of the adoption-revelation process was a search for my biological parents, and I was asked if I wanted to pursue it. I declined; I stated that I wanted to think that through before initiating contact with my birth-family members. I put that matter on the back burner; I felt that the paperwork had answered my questions. I suppose that my fears trumped my curiosity at that time; I didn't want my world invaded and altered by people I didn't know. I worried I would be disabled if the reality of their identity became a part of my life. My children were very young, and I needed to be fully available for their needs. I feared that a lack of emotional well-being would compromise my ability to parent. So life went on; we got busy living.

In 1997, my husband was offered another job transfer, and we moved to Michigan in March 1998. My husband liked to say that we were working our way around the Great Lakes; we had started in Wisconsin, had gone to Indiana, and had ended up in Michigan. The two older girls were in grade school, and the youngest was a preschooler at the time of this move.

We settled into a great neighborhood in Canton, Michigan, which had lots to do, and we met many friendly neighbors. We found a new church, and I found a new BSF class. It was a blessed time in the life of our family. Our children were growing up, and my faith was digging in.

Chapter 4

Facing Our
Biological Pasts
Exodus 5-14

Moses: Full of faith in my God-given mission, my family and I began our journey to Egypt. I sought out my father-in-law before our departure and asked for his blessing and words of wisdom. He had been such a source of strength and conviction to me that I fully absorbed his words and wrote them on my heart. Just as I had listened to my mother, Jocabed, I breathed in his discernment and confidence in the understanding of God and His ways. They had communicated to me that God never asked us to do what He hadn't equipped us for and that whatever we couldn't do ourselves was His part. He empowered those who are commissioned to do His will. That spiritual power increased with each step I took toward my former home.

As we traveled, we talked and meditated on how God can use us when we least expected it. My sons and their families were faithful believers and a source of unwavering strength to me. We reminisced and laughed as we remembered special times we had shared as a family. Zipporah was aware of my occasional lapses in self-confidence, but in her quiet and loving way, she would minister to my head and heart the unconditional love of a devoted wife who believed in her husband's strength of character and resolve.

As we entered Egypt, I was in awe of how much my former homeland had changed. The vast expanse of the landscape took my breath. I sent one of the members of our entourage ahead to find my brother, Aaron, and he was brought to me. Our reunion was just as I had imagined it would be. My self-conceived idea of becoming the deliverer of my people so many years earlier was a distant memory, and we embraced each other as brothers should.

He escorted my family to his humble home and helped us get settled and fed. We talked about the past we had spent together as well as the years we had spent apart.

I was also reunited with my dear sister, Miriam. She had such an expressive face; I could see each emotion she felt as I shared with everyone why I had returned. I told them about the voice that had spoken to me from the burning bush. I told them that God in all His glory and power had described how He was going to give them the freedom they had been praying for since their captivity began hundreds of years ago. I told them I would go to the pharaoh and tell him God had commanded him to let His people go.

I asked Aaron about being the messenger of God's orders to the pharaoh, and he agreed to accompany me.

Most of the elders of the various tribes of Israel were in favor of the plan I described. The long-suffering of the nation was about to end, and they would experience freedom from the land of Egypt because of God's deliverer, me.

Some of the Israelites, however, doubted that a well-educated former prince who had committed murder and had run away to become a lowly shepherd could have possibly been chosen to do the greatest work their nation had ever seen. They believed that my having been commissioned by God and having returned after forty years in a distant land was simply preposterous. I hoped that once I stepped into the court of the pharaoh, they would be convinced otherwise.

After worshipping and praying to the one true God, we were given restful sleep and peace. At daybreak, Aaron and I got up and prepared for our confrontation with the pharaoh. I brought my staff because I knew I might have had to miraculously demonstrate the power of the One who had sent me. I felt empowered spiritually. I had a sense in my soul that reassured God's plan to use me to confront the 'god' of this land, the pharaoh.

He was expecting me; his soldiers had heard I had returned the previous day. He was surprised by my boldness in seeking an audience with him. I bowed before him and gave him a sincere greeting. He asked me the reason for my visit, and Aaron said, "The God of Israel has sent Moses to deliver a message. He is the one true God. He has seen the Israelites' suffering and has heard their cries. He sent Moses to you to demand that you let His people go. Moses wishes to take them into the wilderness and celebrate his return by sacrificing to the Lord our God, or He may strike Egypt with plagues or with the sword."

Pharaoh contemplated this request but refused it. Instead, he chose to burden the Israelites further by making their labor more difficult. Instead of having straw brought to the brick makers, the brick makers would have to find the straw themselves but nonetheless keep up the same production each day. The pharaoh's heart was hard; he would not compromise the progress of building his earthly kingdom.

The cruel new order went out to the soldiers, and they conveyed it to the Israelites' foremen. They protested, and one foreman even went to the pharaoh to plead for mercy as their labor was being tripled with the added burden of collecting the straw. This infuriated the pharaoh further, and he evicted the man from his court.

The foreman found Aaron and me and vehemently condemned us for making the Israelites work harder. The slaves scattered to gather the needed straw for the bricks. The people grumbled, and some even hurled their displeasure in the form of angry words directed at Aaron and me. I was overwhelmed by guilt in having made things more laborious for them. Why had God allowed this to happen?

I sought out a quiet, peaceful place where I could pray for wisdom and strength. Why would God not give me victory when I had done everything He had told me to do? My soul cried out to my Lord with much uncertainty. I pleaded to be released from causing His people any more grief. The Lord heard my cry and spoke to me. He told me not to be discouraged; He said His plan to free His people was just beginning. He told me He would grant me grace and mercy as I would be sent back to Pharaoh. He revealed His plan to use power and miracles to soften Pharaoh's hardened heart. The Lord reassured me that in the end, Pharaoh would free God's people; He told me I needed patience, trust, and perseverance.

So I returned to Pharaoh's court. Aaron and I repeated our demand that Pharaoh free God's people. I told him, "Let God's people go." I demonstrated God's miraculous power with my staff. Pharaoh's magicians were able to duplicate the miracle using their sinister powers, however. Pharaoh rejected our revelations of divine power and embraced the demonic tricks of his sorcerers.

I went to him repeatedly to plead for my countrymen's freedom. After each time he refused our liberation, God sent plagues of differing forms to the Egyptian people. The first one was turning the Nile into a river of blood. Every water source in Egypt was affected with the exception of the water the Hebrews used, but Pharaoh was unrelenting.

The second plague was a sea of frogs that invaded every inch of the land. There were millions and millions of them, but Pharaoh wouldn't budge.

After that, there was a plague of gnats followed by a plague of swarming insects. Again, the Israelites' homes were spared from these disgusting creatures.

Next, all the livestock owned by Egyptians was infected with deadly sickness. After that, the Egyptian people themselves were sickened with sores that covered their skin, and they were unable to find relief from the pain and itching.

God also sent hailstones to damage the Egyptians' crops, followed by scores of locusts that devoured whatever was left. Pharaoh was still steadfast in his refusal to free God's people, however.

The ninth plague was a darkness that covered Egypt for three days. It was so dark that the people could not see even their hands in front of their faces.

The final plague was going to be the harshest of all. I went to Pharaoh and pleaded for his mercy and favor. I pleaded for the families of the Egyptians as well as his own family. I warned that God was planning to take the life of the firstborn of every Egyptian family if he didn't let my people go, but he was unwilling to heed this final warning.

I asked God for His guidance and received specific instructions for all the Hebrew families. Each family was to receive an unblemished lamb and care for it for several days. On a designated day determined by God, they were to sacrifice the animal and put the blood on the doorposts of their homes. I told them it was God's way of ensuring they would be protected from the angel of death who was coming.

That night, all of us huddled in our homes. We heard the angel descend on Egypt. We heard the agony of God's judgment; no Egyptian family was spared the death of its firstborn. It was a gruesome, indescribable sound; we prayed for the people of the land and asked God to be merciful and gracious to the surviving family members.

The people who had enslaved us were learning the cruel reality of the suffering they had bestowed on us. The condemnation that Pharaoh had declared on the firstborn sons of Israel had then, by God's sovereign judgment, fallen back on the firstborn of Egypt.

At dawn, I went to Pharaoh to ask him one last time to let God's people go. His heart was grieving; he had been devastated. With a wave of his hand, he granted the release of God's people. I returned to the homes of my people and shared the news with them. Each family rejoiced, sang, and celebrated their deliverance.

We gathered our humble belongings and cherished ones. We praised the God of Israel. As the people of God readied themselves for their freedom journey, I sought out a solitary place to meditate in the presence of my Lord. I was so humbled by His glory, and I honored Him. I prayed with a heart that was overflowing with a spirit of thanksgiving and praise. I emptied my mind of all hurtful memories and received His cleansing of my soul. I needed His infilling; I was about to continue my God-given commission of leading His people to the land of milk and honey. He would be our guide and protector on the long-anticipated return to our homeland. Praise to God!

After each family completed packing, we began walking east. The joyful sounds of freedom were overwhelming for me at times. Instead of being the person with the most important things to say, I became a listener. I heard many stories of dreams and answered prayers. I heard the personal accounts of triumph over tragedy. I heard many tales of generational hope. The inspiration I derived from these testimonies humbled me greatly. Even though these people had lived as slaves their entire lives, they possessed a passion for their God, and I learned that the Egyptian captivity had not resulted in the despairing loss of hope that is likely anywhere severe oppression is active.

As we traveled from Pharaoh's kingdom, we were blessed through God's presence. During the day, He guided us across the land in the form of a massive, tall, and wide cloud pillar, an incredible sight. During darkness, it changed to a vibrant tower of fire.

I was so used to being in God's presence that I sometimes didn't acknowledge the awesomeness of what He was doing. The people followed suit. They had not experienced the fellowship the Lord and I shared, so they didn't have the same level of trust and anticipation I possessed. I didn't need to see Him to know He was there; they, however, needed the physical reminder of His provision. I knew the unseen Lord; they needed the physical evidence that He manifested before them. God revealed His presence through spectacular means.

When we reached the Red Sea, I looked to the west and was frightened by what I saw. Others looked behind us as well, and the people started to panic. Pharaoh's army was closing in to possibly recapture or most likely kill us. I raised my staff and called on God to provide a way of escape. I plunged my staff into the sand, and the sea before me began to move. The waters parted, and dry ground was exposed before us. I called to the Israelites to follow me through the sea. There was a wall of water on either side, but we continued toward the other shore. By faith, the Israelites followed me; by faith, they trusted God to keep them safe; by faith, they trusted they would be protected from the Egyptian soldiers. Many were frightened, but they followed me and crossed over on dry land.

As we neared the opposite shore, we saw Pharaoh's army following us onto the sea bed. We hurriedly stepped toward the distant land, and everyone steadily moved to make room for others. Once the last of the roughly one and a half million Israelites stepped onto the dry shore across the sea, we watched and waited to see what God would do next. As we gazed on the sea of soldiers with murder in their eyes, the Lord caused the mighty walls of water to crash down on them. Once they disappeared beneath the surface of the powerful water, we celebrated our inexplicable escape once again. God's chosen ones were safe and free and had nothing but unhindered land ahead of them. Seeing what the Lord had done for his people was awe-inspiring and redemptive. We had crossed over from death to life, and we worshipped the deliverance God had provided.

Jean: God allows trials in our lives not to destroy us but to define us. This spiritual truth was illustrated to me in a memorable way one night in 1999. I was listening to a teaching about a passage in Deuteronomy 32 that is a metaphor for how God tests our knowledge, faith, and willingness to submit. The picture in verse 11 describes the process that mother eagles use to train their eaglets to fly. When a baby is big enough and ready to leave the nest, the mother nudges it to the edge of the nest (which can be in the crevasse of rocks) and pushes it over. The eaglet falls, and if able, it flaps its wings. The mother is also in the air, and if the baby is unable to fly, she will swoop underneath her precious little one and carry it on her back to regain altitude. Once high enough, she moves in a way that lets the eaglet fall from the safety of her body and descend again. She repeats this process until the eaglet learns to fly independently. What a beautiful picture of a loving parent! Kind of scary but necessary to foster independence and survival.

The trials that come to us throughout our lives can sometimes make us feel we are falling. We question our strength and doubt our abilities, we pray for saving, and we also at times pray that God will lessen the physical pain and emotional suffering that accompany these trials. We can feel alone and hopeless, but eventually, we persevere and reach a place of perspective and peace. Our faith grows, and our reliance on the Lord increases.

Little did I know that one of the greatest episodes of personal trial was about to begin within a matter of a few weeks following this message. God was about to stir up my nest, nudge me out of my comfort zone, and make me fly, but I knew He would be there to catch me.

It was a pleasant Friday afternoon in March 1999. The much-anticipated arrival of spring and warmer weather was upon us, as it was sunny and slightly cool. I had gotten the two older girls off to school and had filled my morning with household chores and playing with my preschooler. I got her settled for her afternoon nap and went to get the mail. I noticed a letter from the Wisconsin Adoption Registry. I read it.

Re: DOB 4/13/60 (Fond Du Lac, Wisconsin)

Dear Jean,

My name is Mary, and I work here in Wisconsin as an Adoption Search Consultant. I operate the Wisconsin Adoption Registry. The Registry is an alternative search resource that allows adoptees and birth parents and/or birth family members to register with us in search of their biological counterpart. We also offer search and support to those in need.

A birth mother registered with us in search of the daughter she birthed on April 13, 1960, in Fond Du Lac, Wisconsin. She was a teenager at the time of this birth. She wanted to keep her daughter and refused to voluntarily terminate her parental rights to her child. The court, however, terminated her rights on the basis that she had no viable means of supporting herself and the child. Nor did she have family support to allow her to return home with the child. Subsequently, the child was placed for adoption.

Though the child was absent from her life, she did not forget that child. She has always wanted to search for her and hoped one day to be reunited. Years have passed, and the child is no longer a child but a woman in her own right. She has a mother, and that is not to be replaced. But there are years of questions that still seek answers, perhaps for both of you. You have realized that it is you she has been searching for these many years.

The reason for contact at this time is not to disrupt or destroy your life, but hopefully to enrich it. A wonderful opportunity exists for you to know your birth heritage and to have a medical history along with a chance to meet and know birth family members who want to meet and know you. Most importantly, to meet and know the woman who gave you life.

I have been asked to write you and inquire if you would be receptive to having contact from her. This is a decision only you can make. We felt that should you want to share this information with your parents, it should be your decision to choose the time and place. Therefore, no one knows that a search has occurred.

Your birth mother presently resides in Indiana. She is willing to share information with you regarding your conception, birth, and subsequent adoption. There are medical concerns that need to be addressed. Would you please contact me Jean and express your wishes regarding this matter?

Sincerely,
Mary
Wisconsin Adoption Search Consultant
Wisconsin Adoption Registry

After reading this letter, I no longer had the ability to breathe without doing so consciously. I was numb. My heart was pounding hard. The only time I had come close to this intensity of distress was the time following the loss of our son. Like Moses, standing before the burning bush, I was being asked to return to the family of my birth and face the reality of who I was.

After a few minutes, I called my husband and asked him if he could come home right away. He was home within a half hour and served as a calming force that ministered to the overwhelming storm in me and helped me contemplate my course of action.

I tried calling Mary about an hour later, but I reached only her voicemail. It was the middle of the afternoon on a Friday, and she was not going to return to her office until the following Monday. I left a message and asked her to return my call. For the next two days, I could not do anything productive; I was paralyzed with fear. I had moments when I thought I would finally be able to fill in all my mental "gaps" of who I was, but mostly I thought about not being psychologically ready to find out my family history.

I filled my time with meeting the needs of my family, and I shared my feelings and thoughts with my parents. It was difficult for them to deal with this as well, remembering that my birth mother had not wanted to give me up for adoption.

On Sunday night, after I had settled the girls into bed, the phone rang. It was Mary. She had heard my voice mail and thought since I probably had children that evening would be a good time for me to talk. She told me that she was glad to have heard from me and that my birth mother knew she was calling me. I had so many questions for her: What was my birth mother's name? Where in Indiana did she live? Was she married? Did she have other children? She answered the questions she could but told me that speaking to my birth mother directly would be the best way to satisfy my curiosity. She asked my permission to call my birth mother and give her my number. I consented, and she asked what time she should call. I said that evening would be good, so we agreed on 10:30 p.m. I waited excitedly.

As I prepared for *the* phone call of my life, I got pen and paper handy so I could write down what we discussed. My anxiety level was maxed, so I knew I would need help remembering the details of our first conversation. The phone rang at 10:30 sharp. I picked it up and said hello.

Her name was Ruth. We exchanged pleasantries, and our journeys into personal discovery began. We both had so many questions and eagerly filled in each other's gaps. I was surprised by the identity of my father; I had gone to school with his children and had even dated my half-brother in junior high for about a month. He was exactly two months older than me, so I concluded that when my birth father had gotten my birth mother pregnant, he was already expecting a child with his wife.

I also learned my birth mother had lived in my hometown for most of her life. She had many regrets about her past and shared some details about my birth. She had never wanted me to be adopted; she had signed documents that released me only into the foster care system.

I learned that when she finished her prison sentence, she married a man who had been one of the guards at the prison. They moved to Chicago, and she tried to create a home environment that would be approved by social services so I could be reunited with her. Those plans became moot when she found she had married a violent man. She had been the victim of repeated physical, psychological, and emotional abuse at his hands.

One day, after they had been married for about eight months, he contracted pneumonia. He went to the hospital and was given penicillin. The doctor who prescribed the antibiotic did not know Ruth's husband was allergic to the drug; he had a catastrophic reaction and died.

Ruth moved from Chicago to her hometown, where she got into trouble again (which was never explained to me) and was sent back to the state prison for women. Her sentence was short, only a few months.

She pursued being reunited with me, but since her father had signed papers that terminated her parental rights, her petition was denied.

At age twenty, she married again. Her husband loved her deeply but was at times very restrictive regarding her interactions with others. For instance, he called the house several times a day to make sure she was there. When he was off work, she spent all her time with him, and he limited her time with family. She told me he was a very jealous man who strove to control every aspect of her life. It was very frustrating for her, and some days it was overwhelming enough to make her dream of being free of him and his controlling ways.

One day, after twenty-three years of marriage, she told him she wanted a divorce and left their home. She had several siblings, nieces, nephews, and some friends. One of her friends offered her a place to stay, so she moved in with her. She filed for divorce and was free.

We talked for several hours and finally hung up around 1:00 a.m. Before we ended our conversation, we discussed the possibility of meeting face-to-face. My husband had a business trip to Indiana during the upcoming week. If I could arrange child care for my kids, I could accompany him, and we could meet during the evening and have dinner. I was thankful one of my friends agreed to take care of my girls so I could go.

We drove to Indiana on a Tuesday afternoon and got settled into our hotel. On the way to our meeting, my husband teased me incessantly about some of my idiosyncrasies (for example, I don't pair up socks—they go into a sock basket, and the girls have to match their own). After the teasing, however, he got serious and said, "If I could have picked a time in your life for this to happen to you, it would be now." He reassured me I was emotionally strong enough to withstand the stress I was feeling. He encouraged me to fuel my emotions spiritually so I would have the Lord's strength and empowerment. He asked me to lean on him if I reached a moment of panic. He reinforced my strength of character and pointed out how they could help me as the evening played out. Most important, he reminded me I wasn't on this part of my journey alone. He told me the Holy Spirit would bless me and help me articulate my thoughts and feelings. He also told me how much he loved me and how much he was anticipating the privilege of watching the reunion.

We arrived at our meeting place and turned to each other. We prayed for the Lord's will and support. After our prayer, we walked into the building. Inside the lobby, we saw two women. We introduced ourselves. I embraced the woman who had given me physical life. We had both brought material resources to enhance the telling of our family histories. We carried these things with us to the dining room. We tucked the pictures under the table and concentrated on looking at each other and sharing the stories of our lives.

My husband, of course, interjected his fondest memories of our life together, and he helped set the tone so I could share at a comfortable pace. My birth mother told me I closely resembled one of her sisters, Myrtle.

The conversation progressed through many stories and personal recollections. It was amazing, but at the same time, my stress level was beginning to climb. My heart was pounding, and I felt flustered. I looked around and was surprised to see we were the only ones left in the dining room. I remember thinking that the restaurant staff would have been amazed by the life-changing event taking place at our table had they known the details of our meeting.

After dinner, we asked for a private meeting room so we could share the pictures we had brought. They accommodated our request, and we were soon sharing an exciting dialog about the major relationships of our lives. My level of stress, however, was still escalating; all I could think of was escaping to a secluded place so I could process the overload of my emotions. I was polite and controlled on the outside, but my inner voice was screaming for me to get out of there.

An hour later, we packed up our pictures and got ready to say good-bye. We made arrangements for my birth mother and her friend to travel to Michigan for my birthday, which was the following month. We finally parted, and my husband and I drove to our hotel. We talked about what I was thinking and feeling and the intensity of my reactions. We thanked the Lord for His presence and strength, and we speculated about what had not been said or asked so we could remember it for our next meeting.

The following day, I took my husband to his meeting and joined a good friend for lunch. She had been my closest confidante throughout the eight years we had lived in Indiana. My oldest and her youngest daughters had been best friends, and we relished the fellowship and sharing.

After our lunch, I said good-bye and called the teaching leader of my former BSF class to tell her about meeting with my birth mother. She invited me over, and I was so thankful to get her perspective and advice as I talked through the events of the previous twenty-four hours. From 1992 through 1998, she had been the voice in my head whenever I studied the Bible. I loved her speaking style and insightful opinions when she taught through my years as a BSF student. Still to this day, I can pick up a notebook of lecture notes and hear her voice. There had been many times throughout the years when I felt I was the only one in the audience because the Holy

Spirit was speaking directly to my heart through her words.

My advice to everyone is to find someone who has the discipline and discernment to be a true representative of the Word and hold onto the spoils of personal study and exhortation. I have heard many sermons, teachings, and lectures, but the messages that inspired spiritual responses in me have been those I remember the most clearly. When a message is prepared with a foundation of truth and love, the result will inspire those who hear it.

I applied many of those life lessons personally, and they have changed the way I approach every relationship. I have been empowered as a wife, mother, daughter, friend, and teacher of God's Word. My spiritual heart, having been prepared, had withstood the emotional storm created by this new relationship. My self-identity had been formed through my active faith and personal growth catalyzed by my BSF education first in Indiana, then in Michigan, and then completing the program following our return to Indiana.

After returning home, I picked up the pieces; I had been transformed by the events of the past several days. I was overwhelmed in one area of my life in particular. I needed to see my mom and dad immediately because I needed to do part of my processing with them and couldn't do that over the phone. They were on vacation in Florida, but after talking to me, they cut their trip short, took a flight back to the Midwest, and drove to my house. It took about twenty-four hours for them to get to me. I was so thankful. Once they arrived, I was able to put myself together and make sense of all the emotions that were scrambled in my soul. They stayed for a couple of days, until I had some clarity about how I was going to process my new reality.

Over the course of the weeks that followed our first meeting, I discovered some very disturbing aspects of my birth mother's life. Her present living arrangement was the most upsetting. She revealed to me that she and her female roommate were "married" to one another and had been together for many years. They, in fact, had been together for a bit longer than my husband and I. They had had a ceremony in front of their families and friends and had made a life commitment to one another. I learned they socialized with many other lesbian couples, and they hoped their lifestyle wouldn't be an obstacle to our newfound relationship.

This revelation was very difficult for me to digest, because I understood the clear teaching of the Bible about all sexual immorality, whether homosexual or heterosexual—it is sinful but forgivable. I kept thinking that I had three daughters to whom I couldn't explain this as a lifestyle acceptable to God, and I didn't want them to think I condoned it. How could I defend my belief in God's Word when it came to their spiritual education on the matter of sexual behavior? How could I blend two very different worldviews and still honor her as my birth mother? Most important, how could I honor my God and Savior in such circumstances?

This conflict raged inside of me. Her partner accused me of being "homophobic," now a predictable response to anyone who disapproves of homosexual lifestyles. I wasn't afraid of them, but I was very cautious about allowing their lifestyle into the fabric of my family life. As they revealed details of their lives and their core group of friends and social activities, I became increasingly less willing to surrender my control over the amount of time my daughters spent with them.

Another aspect of their life was their involvement with a friend who was a Wiccan "high priestess." Wiccan ceremonies took place at night during their camping trips. In addition to that, they were attending women's festivals that included very shocking activities. Because these festivals had security and seclusion from the outside world, they reported that some of the women would go about the day's activities topless. They had communal showers for grown-ups and children together, and that practice didn't happen only during their festivals; this was something my birth mother's partner did with her friend's nine-year-old daughter when she would sleep over at their house. This horrific information confirmed my desire to keep distance between their lifestyle and my children.

I pursued a relationship with my birth mother that excluded her partner and was limited to interactions with me only. This decision infuriated my birth mother's partner, but I would not waver on the matter. I acknowledged that it was a hurtful condition, but I felt I had no other choice given my God-ordained privileges and responsibilities as a mother.

Once the summer of 1999 arrived, I had made sense of the firestorm of emotion that had consumed the spring. I was comforted by the geographical distance between my birth mother and my family. It was a three-hour journey between our homes, so we conversed mostly thru emails and on the phone.

Remember my mention of how the eagle taught the eaglet to fly by dropping it? I was about to be "dropped" again. In late July, my husband told me he had been asked to relocate to Indiana. I was shocked because we had been in Michigan for only sixteen months. My birth mother lived about an hour away from where we had lived before moving to Michigan.

This bump in our family's journey was difficult for me, but we proceeded with the request to return. We contacted our former realtor and set up a trip so we could find a new home. We found the perfect house in our old school district and sold our house in Michigan within four days of listing it.

The first day of school in our new community was starting in the middle of August, but we could not move into our new house until the day after Labor Day. My two older girls were going into fourth and second grade, and I wanted them to start school with their classmates, so the day before school started, the girls and I moved into a bed and breakfast we called home until we moved into our new house.

We settled into our new neighborhood, which thankfully was filled with children. Many neighbors welcomed us to our block, and the transition went as smoothly as it could have.

The smoothness others perceived was not a true picture of my heart's condition, however. I felt vulnerable and exposed being so geographically close to my birth mother. One of my birth mother's nieces had run into the son of my birth father and told him he had a half-sister living in Indiana. I worried about someone from their family showing up at my house unexpectedly and turning my life even more upside-down. I had a plaque on my front door that read, "Friends welcome anytime—Relatives by appointment." It was a necessary mental barrier that eased my worries of additional drama in my life.

When we had lived in Indiana before moving to Michigan, I had experienced so much spiritual growth and had learned to embrace who I was and what I believed about myself. When we moved to Michigan, I had the opportunity for a new beginning when it came to becoming the kind of friend I wanted to be with others, and it was a chance to apply all the spiritual matters I had been learning and was eagerly embracing.

Moving back to Indiana was a time of interacting with old friends, old relationships, old neighbors, and fellow believers while I shook the kinks out of myself. I had regrets about a few of my interactions with others during my previous years of living in Indiana. I had been responsible for three very young children and was stressed and frustrated at times. All of our extended family lived hours away in Wisconsin, and I had some struggles as a mother due to the lack of maternal relationships that could have given me regular positive feedback when I felt discouraged.

It was also during those earlier times in Indiana, before moving to Michigan, that I had transitioned from being a lukewarm Christian to a transformed believer and faithful follower of the Lord, Jesus Christ.

I struggled with my self-identity and my emotional well-being since my world had been turned upside-down since meeting my birth mother. I reunited with some of my former Indiana friends, however, and as time passed, I became less and less crippled by distant memories and started reassembling a life of healthy activity and God-honoring relationships.

The girls got involved in various athletic activities, and we settled into a new church. Bob and I became Sunday school teachers and increasingly became involved in serving our church body. The rhythm of life was chaotic at times, but we just rolled with it. I became involved again in BSF and looked forward to the weekly spiritual discipline and fellowship with faithful women who shared my passion for the Word.

I continued my relationship with my birth mother; we met for lunch once a month or so, and we occasionally spent afternoons talking about our lives. There were other birth-family relatives in Wisconsin who wanted to meet me, so we scheduled a luncheon at a restaurant during the summer of 2000. My parents agreed to accompany me to this luncheon, and we set off cautiously to meet more members of my birth mother's family. Shortly after our arrival, we met an aunt and several cousins. There was some awkwardness, but at the same time, there were fun and exciting moments. My aunt was nervous about meeting me because she had been the one who had refused to take care of me as a newborn. She had lived with shame and guilt for a long time and regretted deeply that her decision not to take me in had caused me physical separation from my family. I told her that I had forgiven her and that she should not worry about my attitude toward her.

After the luncheon, Ruth and I drove around our hometown and showed each other where we had lived at various times in our lives. We talked about the emotional toll of the previous couple of hours. My birth mother had been overwhelmed with emotion after having met my adoptive parents. Once we were on her sister's side of town, we stopped at her house, and I was introduced to additional family members. After that visit, we went to the home of another cousin. I was quickly approaching that slippery slope of overwhelming emotion and heightened stress.

I returned to my parents' home and spent the next several hours processing emotions once again. Meetings like that are extraordinary and draining at the same time. It would be the only time, however, that I interacted with my birth mother's family members.

Over the next year, Ruth and I had our ups and downs. I struggled with spiritual and emotional issues and eventually sought counseling. I had gained a lot of weight—I was "eating my feelings," so to speak. I was terrified of rejecting the woman who had given me life, but at the same time, I couldn't accept her lifestyle choices. Her partner was increasingly pressuring us to expand the width and depth of our social time together; she was threatened by the bond growing between Ruth and me.

We struggled to find common ground; we exchanged emails and had phone conversations that were mutually frustrating. Communication broke down several times, and it seemed that the ends weren't justifying the means.

This roller-coaster relationship became more strained as time went on. We took many breaks, thinking we would make progress and reconnect, but we never found the perfect balance of acceptance.

We drifted over the course of a few years and finally broke communication altogether. It was for the best in my mind. It had drawn me from my responsibilities as a wife and mother, and I didn't want my daughters to have to deal with a damaged Mom, so I left the relationship in the hands of the Lord, and every discernible revelation of His will confirmed that a life apart from my birth mother was His choice as well.

CHAPTER 5

GOD'S SPIRITUAL TRAINING PROGRAM
EXODUS 15-20

Moses: God's people soon forgot their triumphant deliverance from Pharaoh's army. The journey from the Red Sea took the Israelites to a desolate land. The people God had delivered chose not to dwell on His goodness; rather, they grew frustrated and very robust in their complaints. Individuals as well as families approached Aaron and me with their whining and endless moaning regarding their hardships. I became weary of their petitions and tried to reassure the nation that God would provide for their needs.

I sought fellowship in quiet places and pleaded for His merciful hand to meet the needs of the grumbling masses. The Lord God chose to answer my prayers; He sent provision in the form of manna, quail, and water. The manna was found on the ground each morning for every household in each tribe. God sent the water through another miracle that involved me striking a dry area of rock that quite spectacularly produced an unending cascade of delicious, cool, clear water.

We traveled through the desert as God led the way. One day, we were attacked by the Amalekites. I told Joshua to gather men who could defend our people and fight these aggressors. He followed my command and set out to defeat this army of ungodly warriors. I took my staff and climbed to a spot of land where I could observe the war. Aaron and our friend, Hur, accompanied me. I prayed to God to give us victory, and I raised my staff to heaven. I kept my arms raised to empower my men who received God's anointing in the battle.

As long as my arms were raised, our army was winning on the battlefield. I held the staff above my head as the men fought to defend our people. At times, my arms would ache, and I would need to rest them. Each time I did that, the Amalekites soldiers would overpower our troops and we would lose ground. Aaron and Hur found a stone for me to sit on. They stood on either side and held my arms up so we would rebound and regain control of the conflict.

The Lord gave Joshua and his faithful men victory over the Amalekites with their strong swords. After our triumph, I built an altar to the Lord and named it, "The Lord is my Banner." I decreed that my hands were lifted to the throne of God and that the Lord would do battle against the Amalekites from generation to generation.

Following the war, I sent my wife, Zipporah, and my two sons to visit my father-in-law, Jethro. After hearing the story of the liberation of God's people, Jethro accompanied my wife and sons to our desert dwelling. It was a great reunion with my mentor and spiritual advisor

I had loved for so many years. He rejoiced in the work of the Lord in my life. He affirmed me and my leadership.

The next day, I sat to receive the disputes of the people. I was to exact justice for their conflicts and punish those who had offended civility. Jethro observed these proceedings and asked if he could give me some advice. I consented, and he told me I should appoint a group of men to oversee the people and settle their disputes as they arose. The men would act as judges over the Lord's people. He said my time should be spent in fellowship with the Lord so I could meet the spiritual needs of God's people.

I appreciated His advice and acted accordingly; I restructured how we managed the day-to-day needs of the people of Israel. I selected men who had demonstrated qualities of good leadership and instructed them according to God's revelation to me. I taught them God's standards and emphasized how they needed to devote themselves to the principles of God's accountability program that always emphasized a greater degree of sacrifice than that given by those who were not leaders among God's people. They were consecrated to receive anointing for the work of overseeing the issues that arose among the people.

As the people acclimated to this new system of justice, I was able to increase the amount of time I spent with the Lord. I sequestered myself at the summit of God's mountain, and it was there that the Lord communed with me. I carried such a burden for these unfaithful people, and I asked God to increase their faith. They, however, continued to be self-absorbed and panicked the moment their needs were not met. They endlessly doubted the provisions of their Lord. I lifted up offerings and sacrifices to secure the spiritual blessings for the angry and impatient men and their families. I petitioned for their personal deliverance that they narrow-mindedly confused with physically being rescued from Pharaoh's land. I sought God's unending mercy and grace for the people I loved and sacrificially served.

God fellowshipped with me and reassured me He had heard the language of my heartfelt love and devotion for these nomads who suffered from memory deficiencies and spiritual blindness.

I journeyed between the mountain and the people to deliver the words of the Lord. God gave them many directives through me and did many things that showed them His glory and majesty. They worshipped in His presence and tried to understand all His miraculous revelations.

One picture the Lord revealed to me as we communed on His mountain was a description of how He had carried the nation of Israel on eagles' wings and brought the people into His presence. God promised the nation that He would keep His covenant with them and would consider the nation His treasured possession.

One day, the Lord asked me to bring all the people to the foot of the mountain. He asked Aaron and me to ascend the mountain. He manifested His spirit in the form of a cloud and spoke to the masses. The people trembled and feared the voice of God, but they stayed to hear God's words:

> I am the Lord your God, who brought you out of Egypt, out of the land of slavery. You should have no other gods before me.

You should not make for yourself an idol in the form of anything in heaven above or the earth beneath or in the water below. You shall not bow down to them or worship them; for I, the Lord your God, am a jealous God, punishing the children for the sin of the fathers to the third and fourth generation of those who hate me, but showing love to a thousand generations of those who love me and keep my commandments.

You shall not misuse the name of the Lord your God, for the Lord will not hold anyone guiltless who misuses his name.

Remember the Sabbath day and keep it holy. Six days you shall labor and do all your work, but the seventh day is a Sabbath to the LORD your God. On it you shall not do any work, neither you, nor your son or daughter, nor your manservant or maidservant, nor your animals, nor the alien within your gates. For in six days the Lord made the heavens and the earth, the sea, and all that is in them, but he rested on the seventh day. Therefore, the Lord blessed the Sabbath day and made it holy.

Honor your father and your mother, so that you may live long in the land the Lord your God has given you.

You shall not murder.

You shall not commit adultery.

You shall not steal.

You shall not give false testimony against your neighbor.

You shall not covet your neighbor's house. You shall not covet your neighbor's wife, or his manservant, or maidservant, his ox or donkey, or anything that belongs to your neighbor.

The people were terrified when they heard the voice of the Lord, and they asked me if in the future I would speak to them instead of the Lord. I told them they had heard His voice on purpose so they would be cooperative in following God's laws. Reverent fear is a good motivational tool that God uses to influence a spirit of cooperation in His people. It produces an attitude of humility, submission, and compliance that facilitates an attitude of obedience to His Word.

God continued to expound rules and guidelines to us regarding idols and altars, the use of servants, responding to personal injuries, the protection of property, and our social responsibilities.

God also elaborated on His laws of justice and mercy, Sabbath laws, annual festivals, and how He would send angels to guard us and lead us to the place He had prepared for us. The Lord further detailed His responsibilities in the caretaking of the nation when its people were obedient to His laws. Some of these responses were outlined to give comfort, while others were given to serve as warnings. Many of these revelations were illustrated through imagery as well as warnings. He made many statements using the phrases, "If you . . . I will." Let me explain this using some examples: "If you listen carefully to what I say and do all that I say, I will be an enemy to your enemies and will oppose who oppose you" (Exodus 23:22). "If you worship the Lord, then His blessing will be your food and water. I will take away sickness from among you, and none will miscarry or be barren in your land. I will give you a full life span" (Exodus 23:25).

The Lord also spoke of how He would protect us from our enemies and give us victory in battles as we traveled to the Promised Land. Once entering our homeland, He would establish our borders.

One day, He gave me two stone tablets engraved by His hand with ten commands I was to use as a foundational system of accountability to govern the nation. These rules from the Lord were to be handled with reverent care. Each member of the nation would be expected to know the rules, meditate on their meaning, and more important, apply the principles of the rules in regard to their interactions with God and all others. I understood the divine meaning of what the Lord was asking me to teach His people. However, I had consistently observed there was considerable distance between their knowledge of His ways and their personal application of that knowledge. This new covenant with His children would test their obedience and willingness to make Him the Lord of their hearts.

Jean: Our daughters' interests expanded as they progressed through elementary school. They were excellent students and had many athletic interests outside of school. My husband and I were always driving them to and from soccer, volleyball, gymnastics, swimming, basketball, track, dance, Girl Scouts, and academic club activities. Our daughters had many successful experiences, and we attended every game or event with a sense of appreciation for their physical and intellectual gifts.

My husband started coaching a basketball team in which our middle daughter was involved; the team played other elementary school teams in our school district. He had played football, basketball, and baseball throughout his childhood and adolescence and was an accomplished high school competitor, so coaching came easy to him.

At this time in the life of our family, I was witnessing extraordinary spiritual growth in his life and a renewed commitment to Christ that had been somewhat dormant in his life since he had graduated high school. His faith was living and active, and he spent much time listening to the teachings of Bible ministry evangelists on the radio and downloaded from the Internet. He listened to God's Word on audio CDs and MP3s during his thirty-minute commute to work. His favorite teachers were James MacDonald, John MacArthur, and Alistair Begg. He was hungry for spiritual food and feasted through the ministries of his mentors of the faith.

He satisfied his hunger for God's Word not just in his car; he also listened to Bible teaching while taking showers, working in the kitchen, going on walks, doing yard work, on and on. God used his spiritual discipline to mold his character and grow his faith, and he became increasingly bolder in his witness for Christ.

We became involved in a small group in our church. One of our dearest friends shared with me that he appreciated my husband's gift of apologetic teaching (using reasoned arguments in justifying the reality of biblical truth), his consistent approach to Bible study. He was and is a convicted student and teacher, always striving for vertical teaching (that which emphasizes God's relationship with man versus horizontal teaching— that which emphasizes man's relationships with one another. Horizontal relationships with fellow believers are important, but the emphasis of preaching and teaching should begin with vertical focus that leads to spiritual transformation and a right relationship with God, which then leads to and is move conducive to developing deeper and richer relationships other believers) and theological discernment.

On a Saturday morning, December 15, 2001, he woke me up at 4:00 a.m. because he was drenched in sweat and didn't know why. He told me his heart was pounding; he was concerned. The episode passed, however, and he got back to sleep. He got up later to get ready for a basketball game he was coaching. He took a shower, got dressed, and went downstairs to make breakfast for everyone. I jumped in the shower and continued my morning routine of applying makeup and styling my hair. About midway through my preparations, one of my daughters came into the bathroom and said I needed to go downstairs immediately because Dad was feeling very sick. I went into the family room and found him lying on the sofa.

He told me he was experiencing chest pains and was frightened he was having a heart attack. I ran upstairs, threw on some clothes, grabbed my purse, a comb for my wet hair, and the rest of my makeup I hoped I could finish after the crisis was over. I grabbed my keys and helped him into the car. I drove to the hospital in a neighboring town. I called a friend to go to my house and pick up my kids so they could go to her house while we were at the hospital. We called the emergency room to describe his symptoms so they would be ready for us. Twenty minutes after leaving our home, we arrived at the hospital.

He was taken immediately to the ER, and they began to assess his medical condition. After drawing blood and running an EKG, they confirmed he was having a heart attack! My husband was only forty-one then. They were able to stabilize him, and he was admitted to the hospital's ICU. Once he was settled in his room, I began making phone calls. I called our parents, our pastor, and my friend who had my kids at her house. My husband's parents called other family members and drove from their home, four hours away. My prayer partner and some others from our church came to the hospital to support and encourage us because they knew our families lived far away. We were so thankful for their love and support during this intense crisis.

I spent most of that day feeling stressed and frightened. It was a Saturday, and we learned that the heart catheterization specialists were not available until Monday, so we would have to wait forty-eight hours for the procedure that would save my husband's life. Once my husband's parents arrived at the hospital, I went home to explain to the girls what had happened to their dad. They were very emotional and wanted to see him, but I didn't feel they should go because he needed to stay calm and avoid emotional stress.

I stayed with them for a couple hours, but I had to leave after receiving a call from the hospital that his pain had returned and he needed to be moved to South Bend Memorial Hospital, which was bigger and better equipped to handle cardiac emergencies. My response to this news was intense, and I retreated from the people at my house. I went to my office in the basement to cry uncontrollably and pray. After this emotional release, I came back upstairs and got ready to return to my husband's bedside. Bob's parents came to be with the kids, and I drove with a friend to the bigger hospital forty-five minutes away.

Once he was in South Bend Memorial's ICU, he was again stabilized. I got into his room once every two hours for fifteen-minute visits. My friend stayed with me in the waiting room when I wasn't by his bedside.

My husband told me that he could physically feel the prayers of those who knew of his need for healing. When I was at home earlier, I had emailed many friends and relatives about our need for prayer. Our church family was also diligently lifting us up to the Lord in fervent prayers. I was reassured by my husband's experience of spiritual blessing and was encouraged that he felt peaceful rather than anxious as we awaited the medical procedure that would save his life.

Later that night, a twenty-seven-year-old South Bend police officer, Cpl. Ray Wolfenbarger, was rushed into South Bend Memorial's ER. He had been shot on

South Bend's west side while on duty. I learned about his medical condition because I listened to his fellow officers and family members as they gathered in the ICU waiting room. He underwent emergency surgery, and my friend and I were witnesses to the despondency of his coworkers, wife, and extended family. We too got busy praying for the fallen officer.

We learned later that his prognosis was grave; he had very little chance of survival. We witnessed the hope and strength of the Lord while it was proclaimed in that waiting room. The number of people praying increased by the hour, and each subsequent report of his condition was encouraging; he wasn't out of the woods, but he wasn't getting worse. As was the case with my friend and me, they had to wait to know if their loved one would survive the night.

Early Sunday morning, I went into my husband's room to sit with him. He again told me he could feel the prayers of our church family, relatives, and friends in a physical way. He told me he felt reassured that he would survive this trial and that he was heavily burdened to pray for the life of the police officer he could see from his corner of the ICU through some glass walls. He said he had not slept well but had felt the Holy Spirit prompt him to pray for the officer and his family.

Because he was not allowed out of his bed, he had the gift of time. He chose to use his time to pray for someone rather than himself. He felt a connection to Ray Wolfenbarger; he felt divine prompting to lift him to the Lord. This desire to pray for a man who couldn't pray for himself filled my husband with a sense of purpose.

Sunday night, I was encouraged by my husband to go home and get a good night's sleep. His mother was at my house caring for my girls. He wanted me to give them hope that he would recover after the catheterization scheduled for Monday morning. I reconnected with the girls, who were anxious to hear about their dad, the police officer, and the planned angioplasty. After I tucked them in bed, I fell into bed and settled into a deep but restless sleep.

At some point during the night, I had a dream that our son, Austin, and I were together. He looked like my husband when he was a teenager. He asked me to walk with him in a beautiful garden. We strolled, and after a while, we sat on a bench. We looked deeply into each other's eyes. He told me it wasn't his dad's time to join him in heaven. He knew I was worried, and he wanted to reassure me. He told me he loved all of us very much and looked forward to the time we would live together with Jesus. I told him I loved him and missed him very much. He gave me a hug, and I woke up.

That night was the only time I have ever dreamed of our son. I awoke with a sense of peace, and I was very thankful for the glimpse of grace and mercy that the Lord had given me through our visit. I believed Austin had a message for me from the Lord, and he was given the blessing of delivering it to me. I look forward to seeing him again someday in our heavenly home.

Monday arrived, and my mother-in-law and I got the girls ready for school. Once they were on the bus, we drove to the hospital and joined the police officer's family, friends, and relatives in the waiting room. While my husband was having his procedure, we had the privilege of praying with Ray's family and friends. He was still in critical condition, but the doctors were offering glimpses of hope; he was experiencing a miraculous recovery.

My husband recovered as well. After his procedure, the doctor explained that my husband had had two blocked arteries, one of which had been 90 percent obstructed. The doctors implanted two stents to expand his arteries and improve blood flow. The doctor reported that he would be able to go home the next day. We thanked God for his provision and healing.

My mother-in-law and I returned to my house around the time the girls were due home from school. We had a quick dinner, and I took them to the hospital so they could visit their dad. They had not seen him since the morning of his heart attack, and it was a joyous reunion. They climbed into bed with him and listened to him describe the events of the previous three days. He helped them understand why I had to keep them away so he could rest peacefully. He told them he was looking forward to going home the next day and celebrating Christmas with them the following week. We said our good-byes and returned home. As I tucked them in, we said prayers to thank God for His healing.

I returned to the hospital the next morning to drive my husband home. It wasn't until we were on the highway that he released the stress of the previous days. It was a multifaceted release—emotional and spiritual as well as physical. We were so thankful for God's provision and mercy. He had restored our hope through my husband's physical healing, and we also grew closer to each other.

Once you make it through a difficult time, you will have time to reflect and seek understanding regarding the purpose of the challenge and the suffering. I wholeheartedly believe that God uses our struggles not to defeat us but to define us. That is His pattern in Scripture, and it is His pattern in the life of believers.

As I take a moment to reflect on my experiences and how they relate to the story of Moses, I want to contemplate my role of being a God-honoring wife. When the Israelites were attacked by the Amelikites, Moses sought out a place above the conflict so he could witness the battle. He positioned himself and sought God's empowerment and strength through the lifting of his staff. As long as the staff was raised, they were winning. When his arms tired, he needed help to keep his staff raised. Hur and Aaron held up his arms, and God gave the Israelites victory.

Just like Moses, my husband needs me to hold up his arms when the battle intensifies and he is weakened physically or spiritually. I need to be a source of comfort and strength that gives him perseverance when his strength is compromised through illness or circumstances. The Lord will strengthen our marriage through my faithfulness and willingness to carry his burdens when he is facing trials. My husband would do the same for me.

My primary duty as a wife is to serve my husband. His primary duty as a husband is to sacrifice for me and our family. May God be praised for the blessings He bestows on us. He supplies the spiritual nourishment to our souls not to reveal our deficiencies but to demonstrate His power and provision.

CHAPTER 6

WHAT THE LORD REQUIRES
EXODUS 21-33

Moses: Standing in the gap between God and His people was a challenging place for me to be. Most of the time, I yearned to dwell with just the Lord forever and not have to be "Moses the Messenger." His people grumbled and moaned about their hardships in the desert. At times, some even desired to return to bondage in Egypt.

God desired to have personal fellowship with His children, and He gave His laws so people could approach the throne of grace uninhibited. He gave His commands from the throne of heaven to the Israelites to guide and direct their personal accountability so they would be a people set apart from the rest of the world, God's chosen people. They were being asked to consecrate themselves so God could reveal Himself through their faithfulness and conduct. The first four of His laws illustrated how God wanted His people to acknowledge, worship, honor, and obey Him. The remaining six laws addressed their relationships with their parents, their actions regarding

71

the sanctity of human life, their sexual purity, their attitudes toward the material possessions of others, their temptations to be dishonest, and their attitudes of greed.

God loves us so much that He gives us everything we need to be obedient to His Word. God cares about our attitudes and our actions. He articulates in very plain language how He wants to guide us so we can possess His standard of righteousness. However, our sin nature is a formidable foe that wants to wrestle with our spirits constantly.

Matters of the heart are important to God. He wants to be the voice of our minds, wills, and emotions. He wants our submission and surrender so He can occupy the throne of our thoughts, attitudes, and feelings. The only way we can achieve that level of intimacy is to fellowship with Him through meditating on His words and praying to Him with an attitude of humility, repentance, and submission.

Our attitudes and actions, our thoughts and motives, and our devotion and worship matter to God. It may seem to some who do not know God that He is a demander. If that were so, we would not have free will and the opportunity to choose. He is a commander who wants to lead, instruct, and transform our wills. In His divine wisdom, He has offered us a choice to respond to Him. He doesn't force us to follow Him; if that were the case, our faithfulness would be an empty devotion that would eventually lead to resentment and frustration.

God draws us into relationship with Him because He desires fellowship with us. We, the children of Israel, are His chosen ones. He saved us from the spiritual wasteland of Egypt so we would see the height, width, and depth of His glory, power, and love. As I have said many times to the ones appointed to rule over the people, when God says, "Don't," what He is really saying is, "Don't hurt yourself."

Unfortunately, many liberated Hebrews misunderstood that the steps to their ultimate freedom would have to happen within their hearts as acts of faith. We had to divorce ourselves from the Egyptian laws of enslavement and embrace liberation from the idolatry and dictatorship that had governed our lives in captivity.

Once the Lord gave His Commandments in physical form, the stone tablets, He was explicit regarding the care and keeping of His laws. He gave specific instruction on how we were to handle the words of God. He gave us diameters, dimensions, and types of materials. Through His divine revelation, we constructed the place where He would dwell among our nation. Materials were collected from the Israelites. The people gave their treasures and gifts to the Lord, including gold, silver, and bronze; blue, purple, and scarlet yarn; fine linen; goat hair; ram skins dyed red; hides of sea cows; acacia wood; olive oil for the light; spices for the anointing oil and for the fragrant incense; and onyx stones and other gems to be mounted on the ephod and breast piece. Then we made a sanctuary for the Lord to dwell in.

So, the people of the Lord constructed the dwelling place for God and His law. They made an ark, a table, a lamp stand, an altar, and a courtyard. The Lord gave very elaborate instructions regarding the building of His sacred home among the people. He also gave detailed guidelines for the priests and their garments. The priests were consecrated to learn how to care for God's home and were instructed how to make atonement for the sins of the people.

Once His sacred, physical dwelling place was constructed, I returned to the mountain to receive the law. The Lord and I communed for many days, and I received the tablets to take to the holy place among God's people. When it was time to descend the mountain, I was elated to give the physical evidence of God's will written in stone to govern the masses. God gave His divine revelation written in permanence, on stone, so God's blessings could shower the nation. With confidence, I descended the mountain. I walked to God's people with joy and thanksgiving because it had been many days since I had seen them. As I moved to the place where the leadership gathered, I was astonished by what I saw! The people, under the authority of Aaron's leadership, had created a golden calf. Not only had they made it, they were also worshipping it! I was so outraged on behalf of the Lord that I threw the tablets to the ground to demonstrate my fury!

I admonished Aaron; I demanded an explanation. He told me not to be angry because the people were prone to evil. They had asked for a "god" they could worship and see. He also described a miracle that produced the golden calf. He said that everyone threw objects of gold into a fire and the result was the formation of the golden calf!

As I surveyed the throngs of the disobedient, I called out, "Whoever is for the Lord, come to me." The only ones who responded were the Levites, the priests. I ordered them to go out through the people and kill brothers, friends, and others. They obeyed my orders, and about three thousand lost their lives that day.

I told the people I would return to God's dwelling place on the mountain and plead for their salvation.

Once I reached the summit of the mountain, I petitioned for my people. God told me He had blotted them out of His book because of their sin. He sent a plague of sickness that caused great suffering and pain. Once I returned to them, I told them the Lord was sending them from that place where they had sinned against Him. He would send them away because of the promises that He had made to Isaac and Jacob. However, He would not be dwelling among us. Because of their great sin against Him, His desire to destroy them was ever-present. In hearing these words, the people were mournful, and no one put on any ornament; they stripped themselves of any decoration and began moving toward Mount Horeb.

Once our relocation was complete, I set up a tent outside the encampment. It was there that I met the Lord and communed with Him. He manifested Himself as a cloud that would descend upon my tent whenever we met. I inquired about His plan and my commission as the leader of the nation; I asked God whether He was pleased with me; I asked Him to teach me His ways; I pleaded for His anointing and empowerment.

I had emotional and physical pain because of His choice not to dwell among the people. I told him I did not want to move from this place until He had restored our fellowship as a nation. My desire to be a nation that proclaimed His ownership and blessing was my most fervent prayer.

He was pleased with my petition. He restored His fellowship with our nation and people. I worshipped His sovereignty and offered my thankfulness to Him. I also had a request. I asked Him to reveal His glory to me. I knew it was a bold request, but He told me He was pleased with me. He would honor my request. I climbed the mountain once again to await His revelation.

As my anticipation built, the Lord gave me instructions to ensure my survival while I experienced His glory as He physically manifested Himself before me. He told me all His goodness would pass before me and He would proclaim His name. He told me I could not see His face because no one would ever be allowed to see it and live. He directed me to a place among rocks and told me He would put me in the cleft of the rocks and cover my face with His hand until He passed by. Once He passed by, He would remove His hand, and I would be allowed to see His back.

In all His majesty and power, God passed by me, and I was allowed to witness Him in a physical way. I cannot describe this event. I was awestruck and transformed through the Lord's revelation of Himself. I bear witness to His glory that is unparalleled and impossible to comprehend. My God is the greatest physical and spiritual force in the universe. He is the supreme Creator, the sustainer of life.

In that moment, I saw the Lord clearly and had a glimpse of His will regarding everything He had ever done. What I didn't experience, however, was His revelation of the future. That was something no one is capable of knowing; it exists in the heart and mind of God alone. As a result, we must trust and put our faith in His plans for the future. I trust He will consecrate His nation to declare His glory and power.

Jean: Putting my faith in Jesus and trusting in His divine control over my life has been source of spiritual strength for me. Great faith is birthed in the storms of great suffering. The times in my life I experienced the greatest trials were those times I surrendered, submitted, and sorrowed because God wanted to do a great work in my life. He allows hardships because our hearts need spiritual training. The goals are to grow in faith, knowledge, and ultimately application. He repeats these lessons in our lives until we can say, "Been there, done that, know that."

Most of those lessons are repeated because of our stubborn pride. We may even complain as the Israelites did and doubt God's sovereignty and control. However, in moments of honesty, we will admit that God recycles trials to prove we don't know the truth of our spiritual condition, and He is once again giving us an opportunity to demonstrate our understanding of His standard of behavior.

This standard of behavior must translate into our relationships. How we relate to others is one of His chosen battlefields because it has the most opportunities for application of spiritual truth and personal transformation. This area of my life has been extremely challenging. By nature, I am a creature of solitude. I prefer to be alone; that's when my soul gets equipped to interact with the world. I yearn for solitude, revel in it, and am thankful for it. My primary leisure activities and interests are reading and writing, while my secondary interests involve my interpersonal relationships. I enjoy family gatherings, swimming, watching movies, sports, playing games, and volunteering at church. I have been a Sunday school teacher for over twenty years, and I have been a leader in children's ministry. I have been a Bible student and a member of small group ministries.

These secondary interests require social graces, communication skills, hospitality, and a pleasant attitude. I am blessed in those areas, but they are not where my deepest satisfactions reside. In many ways, those areas for personal growth are present because I am a mother of three daughters whose social interests have been much greater than mine. Because I have shared a home with them, my comfort zone has been reshaped and challenged by their social interactions. I have been interactive as they have entertained, but I don't yearn for constant socialization. They don't always appreciate all the details involved in socialization, including snack and meal preparation, buying soda, and general "company-ready" cleaning. My reward for having an open-door home has been great despite my grumbling emotions (never expressed to visitors).

My girls are young adults now, attending college and starting careers and life-long relationships. Many of the kids we "entertained" over the years have come back to say how they were blessed through the interactions they had with my husband and me. We offered a balanced home, a place of peace and acceptance.

Our general approach to parenting has been primarily grace-based, and we disciplined in a spirit of accountability and instruction. Our relationship with our daughters never diminished because of the bad choices they made; we dealt with each offense against our rules in a way that taught them God's standards, and we strived for them to understand that we are all accountable to God for our behavior. They felt the genuine concern and care we offered, and they appreciated that we lived our faith openly and inspired them to become faith seekers too. I believe our approach to parenting made our home a comfortable place for them to express themselves and to entertain friends.

The salvation journey for our daughters at times was challenging, mostly because they struggled with the focus of youth ministry at the church we attended through most of their teen years. The youth pastor and the senior pastor focused on "horizontal" messages aimed at improving the quality and quantity of relationships with others in the church. They used an approach that they hoped would grow and deepen the faith journey of the youth through social interactions, music, and the general sharing of faith stories with the body, human stories meant to inspire and convict the audience of God's grace, mercy, and compassion. Those were good things to offer as an occasional illustrative tool.

However, the pastor's overemphasizing these types of messages hindered the church's spiritual growth. The leadership chose a dynamic of relationships with others and then expanded on man's opinions rather than offering the Lord's instructions through the Bible. This superficial and shallow presentation of the philosophy of human ideas was stifling to hear throughout our years there. My husband and I were active in teaching (me in children's ministry and he in adult ministry), and we belonged to a small group that met weekly; that was where our faith walk was challenged and we increased our understanding of Scripture. We were very close with our group, as we all immersed ourselves in the discipline of Bible study and responding to the call to service in the church body. This is how we were able to tolerate all that was lacking from the pulpit, but we did grieve over these issues for a long time.

We met with the church elders and shared our concerns but were told nothing would change. We pointed out that other people shared our opinion, resulting in a population of seasonal seekers who left to find solid biblical teaching elsewhere. Being a "transitional" church was okay with the leadership we talked to, however. The leaders didn't want the pastors to be overburdened with preparing in-depth, biblically sound teaching because it would be time spent away from their families and fellowshipping with the congregation.

We presented all our suggestions and encouragements in an atmosphere of love and mercy. Their responses to our concerns caused such deep spiritual pain that we felt we had no choice but to leave that church.

The spiritual training of our daughters was a responsibility my husband and I took very seriously. Despite their resistance to the methods of teaching in their former youth group, they all made a public proclamation of their faith and chose to be baptized. Each daughter made her commitment while in middle school. The nurturing of their living faith was a priority for us as parents.

I had taken them to BSF throughout their preschool years. When they were in elementary school, I switched to evening BSF classes to which they accompanied me. My husband went for four years, and our middle daughter went with him. Those seeds of faith that had been routinely sown in our weekly schedule from their earliest years became tools the Holy Spirit used to shape their worldview. They participated in worship, Bible study, prayer, and group discussion.

At times, however, the program was overwhelming for them as they became reluctant to be transparent through the sharing of spiritual ideas (mostly in the middle of their elementary school years). I believe the Lord gave them a foundational understanding of biblical truth and its application to their daily lives.

The study guides we prepared at home were tools that prompted group discussion and debate in our family. It became a natural dialog in the language of our interpersonal interactions as well as a topic of discussion with their friends who regularly visited our home.

I once heard in a BSF lecture the "key" to Christian parenting: it's not the church you attend, it's not the programs you're involved in, it's not the concerts you take your kids to, it's not the books you read on parenting, and it's not found through various forms of media. The key that determines your success or failure as a parent is the amount of time you spend in fellowship with the Lord through prayer. You must get as close as you possibly can to the heart of God. He shapes thoughts that lead to words,

words that lead to actions, actions that lead to habits, and habits that lead to victories in malleable hearts.

We all have heard children emulate what we do, not what we say. I have found that when parents seek the foundation for daily decisions from the heart of God, they are enabled and equipped to shape their children's spiritual hearts (their minds, their wills, and their emotions). These were the spiritual truths not presented in our church's youth group. The principles and applications that should have been included in weekly sermons were also absent. It was a horizontal rather than a vertical fellowship. We yearned for a church that emphasized the latter.

The greatest trial we faced as parents of teenaged girls was when our youngest daughter was fifteen. She had met a young man from a neighboring town while visiting a youth group activity with one of her friends. He seemed nice and generally well-balanced, and he was good looking, but as she dated this boy, we saw that he had some emotional and psychological issues. Over the course of several months, we noticed our daughter was becoming stressed and depressed. We shared our concerns with her and prayed for them both. Every time she talked to him on the phone, she would isolate herself and cry because of the things he had said. She shared with us that he was depressed, suicidal, and having psychotic episodes. She cared for him deeply and had much compassion for him. He told her that she was the only one who cared about him and that he didn't have anyone else to turn to. My husband and I also reached out to him. We had our concerns, prayed for his healing, and encouraged him to reach out to his pastor and youth leaders.

One evening, he was at our home, and our daughter came to us with great concern for him. She said that while they were watching a movie, he started dozing, and she had had a lot of trouble waking him up. My husband and I went to see if we could help him; he was lethargic and had limited verbal responses to our questions. His parents were due shortly to pick him up, so we helped him stand and walk to the door. His mother and sister pulled into our driveway just as we helped him sit down on the steps. I went to their car and described his current condition; his mom told me to call 911. The paramedics were at our home within a few minutes. His mother described a seizure condition that her oldest daughter had, and it was determined he was also experiencing a seizure. He was taken to the hospital for evaluation, received medication, and was released later that evening. The evaluations confirmed a seizure disorder. This diagnosis led to further medical interventions to deal with his depression, suicidal thoughts, and hallucinations.

After these serious problems were addressed, we asked our daughter to end her relationship with him. We felt it was his family's responsibility to care for him and address his issues without the complications of having a girlfriend he strove to control and manipulate.

While she was in the relationship with him, her stress level was high. It was affecting every area of her life, and she was in a state of emotional upset twenty-four hours a day, feeling responsible for his well-being.

Throughout the crisis that followed his seizure, he became even more manipulative, and he told my daughter many lies about his home life. He threatened suicide because of our request for her to end the relationship.

Reluctantly, she broke up with him. The following week, while she was playing soccer at a park near his house, he attempted to take his life by swallowing a bottle of pills. He told his dad what he had just done and waited for the ambulance to arrive, knowing our daughter would see it and become distraught.

His suicide attempt did get her attention, and we reluctantly took our daughter to see him at the hospital so she would know he had survived. We allowed a visit but did not approve any communication between them. He was sent to a psychiatric facility for two weeks following his suicide attempt. My husband and I asked his parents to help prohibit him from not communicating with our daughter.

On the day he returned to his parents' home, he was left unsupervised, and he called our daughter. He told her he had failed the first time but wouldn't make the same mistake twice. He wanted her to continue the relationship even though both sets of parents wanted it to end. I took the phone from my daughter and asked him to let me talk to his parents. After arguing with him and threatening to call the authorities, he relinquished the phone, and I talked to his mom. I told her I would get a restraining order if she couldn't prevent him from contacting my daughter. She took my threat seriously and assured me he would not contact our daughter again.

The progression of actions we took to handle the dissolution of this unhealthy relationship was a trying process. At first, we prayed for her to end the relationship on her own and protect herself. Then, we offered suggestions regarding what we had observed and how it was affecting her emotionally. We encouraged her to speak to his pastor (she regularly attended his youth group and was close to the youth pastor) and have him suggest to his parents that her ex-boyfriend needed additional help.

Sometime later, after this relationship was in the distant past, as we were reflecting on some of the things that had happened, I learned from one of our daughter's close friends just how desperate he had been to control her. She told me that she and my daughter had bought tickets to see a play at a neighboring high school. Once seated in the theater, our daughter started getting texts from her boyfriend expressing his disapproval of her being there; he actually told her to leave. She kept texting him that she was enjoying herself and wasn't the one who had driven them to the school, so she couldn't leave without her friends going too, which she didn't think was fair. He sent her a picture of a large quantity of pills and texted that he would take them all if she didn't leave the play.

She came home twenty minutes after that text and went to her room, closed the door, and cried herself to sleep. We asked what had happened, and she told us she didn't feel well. I tried to talk to her, but all she could do was cry. This trial was extremely difficult for us as a family, but it was a time the Lord used to teach our daughter the extent of our commitment to protect her, love her, and encourage her to make healthier relationship choices.

Our oldest daughter had many moments throughout her late adolescence when she struggled with the level of accountability that Christians accept when they make commitments to Christ. She struggled with the focus of the youth group as well as the transparency of self-assessment. She told me many times she did not want to submit to an authority that examined and exposed spiritual weaknesses. My husband and I prayed that she would have a personal encounter with God to enable her to find a faith that was personally transformational and real. I told her that God uses our trials to confirm our faith and make us stronger. He allows circumstances that challenge us because His deepest desire is for us to reach out for His strength and protection. I advised her to be cautious in her struggle with submission because the Lord may allow something catastrophic to occur in her life that could bring her to her knees, as was the case with me when I denied Jesus' lordship over me in my twenties. He had called to me from my brokenness to transform me into fellowship with Him again.

Our second-oldest daughter graduated from high school in 2010. She has always been very self-directed and passionate about her life decisions. She had many positive experiences throughout her high school career. She graduated first in her class with a 4.0 and received a tremendous scholarship to college. One of her main academic interests in high school was German. She told us she wanted to move to Germany to work for a year following her graduation. She found an organization that helped young adults wanting to travel and work in Germany and received contact information for a family with two small girls. She communicated with the parents

and reached an agreement to work for them as an *au pair,*
a nanny.

She asked her college to defer her scholarship for a
year, which it agreed to do. Three days after she graduated
from high school, she flew to Germany with an agreement
to work for her host family for a year. This, of course, was
a faith journey for us as parents; we wondered if we were
doing the right thing. We put our faith and trust in the
Lord as well as our daughter, however, and we prayed
daily for her well-being.

Her experience was very positive. She immersed
herself in the language and really loved her host parents
and their children. We spoke with her often on Facebook
and Skype. Our oldest daughter missed her terribly and
asked to visit her during the Christmas holidays in 2010.
We agreed to this trip and made reservations for her
flights.

Our daughter in Germany was given an old VW
Beetle to drive while she was working for her host family.
She fell in love with that car and talked about getting one
for herself after she returned. She went to the Frankfort
airport to meet her sister and learned that due to bad
weather, her sister's flight had been diverted to Munich.
Our oldest was offered bus transportation to Frankfurt
and arrived there many hours later. She was very anxious
about the changes but prayed for the Lord to keep her safe
and reunite her with her sister.

Once they found each other, they walked to the old
Beetle and loaded the luggage. They were, however, not
prepared for what happened next. The car was dead. Our
middle daughter called her host dad and asked him what

to do. He told them to try slamming the driver's door as they turned the ignition key. He also told them to have our oldest daughter bounce up and down on the back of the beetle (where the engine was) and turn the key.

Before they tried these somewhat ridiculous ideas, they prayed for success; they were feeling quite hopeless. After praying, they opened and slammed the door of the vehicle, and the car started! They were able get back to the host family's house.

The bus ride to Frankfurt was the first spiritual victory for them, and the car's revival was the second. Seeing faith in action is very convicting, especially when you're struggling to see physical evidence of answered prayers. My husband and I prayed that a spirit of conviction was birthed in them through their trial, and we thanked the Lord for their safety.

One week later, they had a second adventure that challenged their faithfulness and submission to spiritual intervention. They had always dreamed of going to Paris, so after Christmas celebrations with the host family, they traveled to Paris to celebrate New Year's Eve. Once again, they relied on the old Beetle and had a wonderful time driving through southern Germany and northern France.

They were on the north side of Paris when the car died at a stoplight. They were able to push the Bug to the curb, and they called the host dad for his advice. He reminded them of the car-revival strategies and wished them luck. They prayed for another miracle. As they were assessing their surroundings, they saw girls standing on the sidewalk across the street who were getting into and out of cars. Realization struck—they were in Paris's red-light district. They prayed again and tried to get the car running, but it wouldn't start. Their faith was being tested; they prayed for help in the form of a rescuer who spoke English or German because neither knew any French.

Our middle daughter found tire chains in the trunk. She stood by the back of the car, near traffic, and swung them over her head to alert other drivers that they needed assistance. In a short time a nice, middle-aged man pulled up behind them. He spoke English. He offered to tow them to their hotel (on the other side of Paris) and helped them find a mechanic to look at the car!

He towed them to the hotel and helped them get the car parked in the garage. He accompanied them to the check-in desk and explained to the clerk their need of a mechanic. The arrangements were made, and they expressed their sincerest appreciation to him and said good-bye. Once again, their faith had proven to be living and active, and they were in awe of the power of prayer. They praised the Lord for His protection and provision.

These experiences so convicted our older daughter that she began to rest and rejoice in the presence of the Lord and put her faith in His reassurance.

I received a phone call from them about their adventure, and they reassured me they were safe. I was very thankful for not having known what was happening in "real" time. They celebrated the New Year with an increased awareness of the Lord's love for them, and more important, the car was repaired for their return trip.

The most challenging events of our lives as parents were behind us; the Lord helped our children find their own strength and personal faith through trials. We became increasingly aware, however, that we had to examine the focus of our hometown church and moved closer to a decision to transition to a new fellowship of believers. As I had written previously, my husband and I had been disciples of James MacDonald's radio and Internet teachings for many years. He is the senior pastor of Harvest Bible Chapel, a Chicago church ministry. We discovered a church in a town about a sixty-minute drive from us, but we knew without a doubt that it, a Harvest Bible Chapel, would offer sound biblical teaching.

We attended a Sunday morning worship service there in August 2011. Our primary concern with our previous church had been an absence of vertical preaching, but the Harvest Bible Chapel pastor gave a convicting message and even used the word *vertical* several times during his message. We felt the Lord's blessing on our future affiliation with this biblically principled church and became members in November 2011.

Throughout my journey as a Christian, I have been blessed with a vibrant faith, a growing knowledge, and a passion for teaching God's Word. In our new fellowship of believers, I felt a different nudge from the Holy Spirit. Making the transition from one church to another had been so emotionally and spiritually draining for me that I felt an overpowering need to recommit to the Lord through baptism. My first baptism had followed confirmation class when I was around fifteen. It was a "sprinkle" baptism, with just my head being wetted by the minister's hand. I have no doubt that I became alive spiritually on that day in 1976, but I felt led to redo my public confession of faith and experience baptism through total immersion.

In the previous twenty years, I knew I needed to repeat my baptism to experience the "public proclamation" with total immersion, but I delayed it mostly because I didn't want to be seen with wet hair and dripping makeup. I convinced myself to suppress my vanity and recommit to Christ and our new church body. So, on February 19, 2012, I shared my faith story and was baptized through immersion. It was an outward expression of the inward action of being saved by grace through faith in my Lord and Savior, Jesus Christ.

Throughout the previous decade, I had worked at a Brethren church as a preschool teacher for children from three to five years old. It was a very rewarding ministry; I was able to live out my faith in a way that gave children a spiritual foundation and basic understanding of God's Word. We used a Bible curriculum and expounded scriptural principles through Bible stories. Presenting biblical truth in a fun and interactive way was very meaningful for me. I especially enjoyed engaging the children in music and storytelling. I have very few inhibitions when it comes to being around children, and I enjoyed playing and purposeful activities alike.

I left that job in the fall of 2012 to pursue writing this story. I had been nudged for the past five years to write it, but I had put it on the back burner, so to speak, because of a busy family life and a love for preschool teaching.

I have learned, however, that when God has a job for you, you need to submit to His calling. If you ignore Him, you will eventually reach a point that He rearranges your schedule so you don't have a choice but to follow His plan. That is how He worked my circumstances—I had postponed the task, and as a result, He changed my vocation and calling.

CHAPTER 7

GLIMPSES OF GLORY
EXODUS 34-40

Moses: Following my physical encounter with God, I was overwhelmed and moved spiritually as I yearned for a continuation of fellowship with Him. I had met my Lord many times, but actually seeing His glory manifested before me prompted my desire to celebrate His revelation and bask in His presence.

Of course, He had other plans for me. He commissioned me to gather two stone tablets and return to Mount Sinai alone. He was to meet me there and chisel His commands into the new stones. I complied and returned to our mountain to receive God's laws. Once there, He used His omnipotence to reproduce an identical set of Commandments for me to deliver to the people.

The Lord and I communed for forty days and nights. During that time, I did not eat or drink; all of my needs were met by the Lord. He fellowshipped with me and revealed His plan to manifest His power and glory among the people. He gave many directives regarding the care and keeping of His Word. He was very detailed in His requirements for the people to atone for their sins. He gave me His future instructions for the nation regarding worship and sacrificial giving. He repeated His promises to grant His people victory over every enemy. I thanked Him for His mercy, His forgiveness, and His many blessings. I thanked Him for the grace He had bestowed on me to be His spokesperson and servant. He is the one true God; may His name be forever praised!

Once I returned to the people with the new tablets, some viewed me with astonished stares and gasps, and that startled me! Apparently, my face was luminously radiant due to my encounter with the holy manifestation of God. To settle their fears and uneasiness, I started wearing a veil whenever I was in their presence but would remove it when I communed with God.

The people received me and listened attentively to my instructions. I had the stone tablets I had received from the Lord, and I had the details for the construction of His physical dwelling place among us. When the people heard my directions and understood the information regarding God's holy temple, they responded by providing many of the materials they had carried from Egypt. Everyone sacrificially gave from his or her possessions, and they joyfully followed my detailed cognitive blueprint.

Each person who served beside me was a blessing to me. The people responded with fervent workmanship and devotion. In time, we completed our task. The Lord would soon have a holy, sacred dwelling place among His people. His laws would govern the masses, and His Spirit would guide us. The Lord was pleased with what we had accomplished according to His Word.

Jean: God's dwelling place among the Israelites was prepared in great detail with reverence. For me, God's dwelling place is in my heart, which is His home, so I need to be diligent in preparing it for His Spirit, protecting it for His Spirit, and producing fruit for His kingdom. My spiritual heart has been described to me as being the origin of my mind, my will, and my emotions. My thoughts matter to God. My attitudes matters to God. My feelings matter to God. My spiritual heart needs protecting and equipping; I need to guard it from the enemy of God, Satan, who loves to hinder the spiritual heart through mind games, temptations, doubts, and fears. He loves to penetrate our circumstances and manipulate us so we take our focus off that which matters to God, including integrity, honor, truthfulness, trustworthiness, and service for the kingdom. He wants us to sin, resulting in separation from fellowship with God. Our minds, our wills, and our emotions are his playground, and he is constantly feeding us a steady diet of lies and deceit.

God allows these attacks because they grow our dependence on Him. He will defeat the evil monster in His time, but meanwhile, we must guard our hearts and feed them a steady diet of biblical truth. We must pray and protect our connection to God so we will be equipped to live faithfully. The ultimate battle is the Lord's, but we must not give Satan a foothold to separate us from the Lord's kingdom. In this world, that can be easier said than done, but we should lay our lives down daily and press on, knowing we are the hands and feet of the Lord's ministry.

I want to revisit the subject of family. Usually, the greatest celebrations and challenges in this life occur in the context of our closest relationships. The greatest joys and the deepest sorrows are birthed in the most vulnerable places. I was vulnerable from the earliest moments of life because I had been a ward of the state placed in foster care. From the first moment they held me, my parents were loving and nurturing. I had come into their home as a foster child, so from one day to the next, they didn't know if they would be able to keep me. The circumstances of my birth were complicated because my birth mother had been in prison when I was born.

My parents received details about my birth family because of the risk my birth family might have discovered my whereabouts and have been forceful in reclaiming me. It was unusual at that time to have many details about the circumstances of a foster child. Because my birth mother was trying to get her parental rights reinstated, my identity needed to be protected. This volatility was a constant concern for my adoptive family; they desired to protect me at all costs.

One day, when I was about seven months old, the state wanted to give my parents a baby who had some medical problems and move me to a different home. My parents refused to consider this change of circumstance, however; they had expressed a desire to adopt me and already thought of me as their own. I am grateful they stood their ground and adopted me.

My relationship with my parents was challenging during my adolescence, but their love for me has never wavered. My parents are two of my closest confidantes. They have supported me through every phase of my life and tell me regularly how proud they are of me as a mother, a sister, a daughter, and a wife. They deeply respect my husband and me and have bestowed many blessings on our family. Have we made mistakes and carelessly hurt one another? Yes, occasionally, but the foundation of our relationship has never been rocked. It's been a great source of strength and a model of behavior we have talked about many times with our children. The strength of the family is the foundation of society. It was designed by God to be the healthiest and most rewarding way to raise children, and it is the source of generational blessings. I love them very much.

My husband's family has also demonstrated the benefits of being committed to one another. My in-laws are extremely generous and attentive in their relationships, and they cherish each member of our family and always offer encouraging words. They are very affirming and strive to bless others because they have been richly blessed. They wear their joy and strength of character as they age, and they seek to share their love and hospitality with dignity and grace. I love them very much.

Previously, I wrote about my day with my birth mother's family members and how they affected my life. I want to talk now about my birth father's family. After I had gotten in touch with my birth mother, I pondered exploring my birth father's life and wondered about his family. I prayed to the Lord and asked him for guidance.

I longed to see a picture of my biological dad, and I wondered how many half-siblings I had. God did not prompt me to seek a meeting with him or his family, but he gave me something else in June 2007.

My parents called me once with news of the death of a neighbor, the mother of one of my closest childhood friends. I grieved her passing and had many happy memories of spending time at her house. After our conversation, I went online to look up her obituary. As I scrolled through the death announcements, I saw my birth father's name and clicked on the link. At the top of his obituary was his photo, and I read about his life. His memorial service was to be held in a couple of weeks at a chapel in town. I went to the chapel website and read more about him and saw additional pictures. I learned I had seven half-siblings, a few of whom lived in Alaska, in Juneau. I have a brother who lives in Anchorage. It was very interesting to learn this, and I was thankful to the Lord for honoring my prayer to get a glimpse into his life and finally to have an image of my birth father.

My responsibilities as a mom have been changing; our youngest graduated from high school this spring (2013) and will be going to college in the fall. My role as a mother will change. My interactions with my college-aged daughters will become increasingly electronic—cell phones, emails, and Facebook, and my husband and I will transition into a new schedule with a lot less activity. However, I look forward to the new defining moments the Lord will provide to draw me closer to Him. He will equip me to do new and exciting things with the extra time that comes from being an official empty nester.

It is the hope of my heart that you have grown in your faith because of reading our story. Remember, God can use a government (Pharaoh, the State of Wisconsin, and so on) to determine where we are born and grow up. He can use our transgressions to bring us to the place of humility; that is where He does His greatest work. He can use our most serious offenses and transform our hearts so we help those who are suffering through great trials. He can break our hearts to the point of surrender that only He can save us from. He can fill us with His Spirit so we can do His will on earth. We carry on so one day we can come face-to-face with Him in our heavenly home and hear the words, "Well done, good and faithful servant." May His name be praised!

CHAPTER 8

VISIONS OF THE PROMISED LAND
EXODUS 40:34-38, DEUTERONOMY 34

Moses: God was pleased with all our hard work when we finished His temple. He was to come down and dwell with His children, the nation of Israel. We prepared His dwelling place and awaited His arrival. He would lead us to the Promised Land, and our triumphant return was to be realized because He would accompany us and give us victory over every nation as He had proclaimed.

He promised to continue His fellowship with me, and I was humbled to be called a servant of God Most High. His revelation of Himself and His requirements for worship and service would continue as we stepped out in faith. The Lord would send us out of this land to proclaim His glory and sovereignty so other nations in the world would see His blessing on us.

For the forty years following our deliverance from Egypt, my time and energy were consecrated to the Lord, and I continued to be the spiritual leader of our nation. The Lord would require much from His people, and I would instruct them in the Lord's ways.

The Lord gave us many ways to demonstrate our devotion to Him. He commanded that we establish ceremonies, laws, and festivals to worship Him. The priests oversaw the temple of God. My brother, Aaron, supervised these men and taught them the ways of the Lord. God had given much to the nation of Israel and demanded much in return.

I led the nation of Israel for many years. When we approached the Promised Land, only Joshua, Caleb, and I were left of the original people who had left Egypt. I think the Lord wanted to prolong our time in the desert so the memories of our captivity would be forgotten and the old generation that had experienced the bondage of slavery would die out, resulting in a new generation of Hebrews that would not doubt His sovereignty, provision, and lordship.

Before my death, the Lord chose Joshua and Caleb to lead His people physically into the Promised Land. Just as the Lord had trained me, I trained Joshua and Caleb for their task of leading the nation to the land future generations would call home.

The Lord did not allow me to physically enter the land He planned to give to the nation. He requested that I return to our mountain for our final time of fellowship while I lived in this world. He graciously gave me a vision of the land my people would call home. After this revelation, I peacefully left the earth to join Him in heaven. May His name be praised throughout the earth, and may you be drawn to Him through the time we have shared as I described my experiences recorded in the Holy Scriptures.

Your salvation is important to me, and I hope you have been moved to explore a vibrant, personal relationship with the Lord. He is waiting for you to respond to His voice. I pray you allow Him to sit on the throne of your heart so you can experience the freedom He wants to bless you with. He is your heavenly Father, too, and He is looking forward to fellowship with you. May His name be forever praised!

Jean: The deepest desire of my heart is to be a witness to the lordship of my Savior, Jesus Christ. When He is invited to accompany believers through the trials and blessings in life, they can walk with confidence and assurance that they can make a difference in the lives of those they encounter along the way.

Epilogue

Dear reader,

Inviting the Lord to sit on the throne of your heart is life-transforming. Jesus came to be a sacrifice for you, and He paid the ultimate penalty for your sins. He died on the cross to pay the ransom God required as payment so you can have the assurance that through your confession of sin, sincere repentance, and proclamation of Him as your Lord and Savior, you will receive the gift of eternal life.

When you become a believer, the condemnation you deserve will be removed from your eternal life so you can dwell with the Lord forever in heaven after your physical death. Are you willing and ready to receive the transforming grace, mercy, and forgiveness God offers to all believers? Here are some suggestions for you to consider as you explore the process of receiving salvation through the life, death, and resurrection of Jesus Christ:

1. Purchase a Bible. Before you open it to read, pray to the Lord for understanding and revelation as you read.
2. Find a place of worship that unapologetically proclaims the truth of God's Word—a place that

offers discipleship training so you will grow your faith, a place that offers meaningful ministries that put you in contact with mature Christians who can nurture and support your growth as a transformed child of God.

3. Strive to examine areas of your life where Christ needs to reshape your heart. To discern the Lord's will, you must develop the discipline of prayer, which is conversation with the Lord. It is a time for you to talk to Him and listen to Him. God speaks to us in several ways: through the revelation of Himself in Scripture, through prayer, through our circumstances, and through other believers.

4. Once you establish yourself in a community of faith, sign up for a baptism class and participate in the public proclamation of your decision to become a disciple of Christ. I recommend being baptized through total immersion.

5. Following your baptism, explore the commitment of the church's membership. The pledge of membership in the body of the church is a way to create a system of accountability for believers to support the ministries of the church of Jesus Christ. Additionally, membership enhances the responsibility to participate in providing financial resources to enhance the effectiveness of the church as it reaches out to a broken world in constant need of salvation. Financially supporting your church and its ministries helps the global church grow and reach out to the worldwide ministry of Jesus Christ.

6. Following your baptism, become a member of a Bible class to grow your understanding of God's Word. After achieving a better understanding of God's Word, look for opportunities to serve within the church body. Most churches offer a list of areas for service. Choose one, and start doing the Lord's work in a way that blesses others.

I pray you have grown in faith and knowledge to the point of looking for your own story in the Bible. It is one story, God's story, and it can transform your life and make you a powerful witness to His love, grace, mercy, and redemption.

I would like to share with you what I once heard at a women's retreat that had a profound effect on me. The speaker asked us about our favorite authors—their names, where they lived, whether they were already deceased, and if we had ever had personal contact with them. She explained to us that studying the Bible is unique when compared to reading any other book; it is different because every time you open it, the author is present and willing to answer questions, give insights, and grow your understanding of His Word. No other author can offer that.

Blessings to you as you seek your own story from the pages of God's Book, the Bible.

Acknowledgements

I wish to personally thank the following people for their contributions to my inspiration and knowledge and other help in creating this book:

-Jesus Christ: Jesus, you gave me a vision five years ago to write this book. Your name is not in the title, but your Holy Spirit has dwelt in my heart and given me the wisdom and discernment to tell the story of your transformational power and healing in my life. You are my Savior, Lord, and friend. I love you.

-Bob Schultz: Throughout the past twenty six years of marriage, you have supported and encouraged me with a spirit of patience, understanding, and love. The past year has proven to be a test of strength, perseverance, and devotion on your part as you have waited for the fruit-bearing of my vision, especially the past eight months while I dedicated my time and focus to writing. Your editing, revising, and feedback have been invaluable to me and your contributions have been insightful and appreciated. I love you and look forward to partnering with you throughout the remainder of our lives as we minister on behalf of our Lord and Savior, Jesus Christ.

-Madeline, Katherine, Jessica: Thank you for your prayers, encouragement, and permission in allowing me to speak truthfully and transparently about the life experiences shared as a family that illustrated your faith journeys and personal transformation into faithful followers of Jesus Christ. Your Dad and I couldn't be more proud of the women you have become and we anticipate with joy and thanksgiving your continued spiritual growth and service in the name of the Lord, Jesus Christ. I love you very much.

–Matt and Chad: Having each of you join our family as son–in–laws is such a blessing to Bob and me. You both have demonstrated your willingness to love deeply and serve sacrificially as husbands, as well as disciples of the living God. You are loved and adored and I couldn't imagine our family without you. Bob and I both look forward to witnessing your spiritual growth as Christians who impact the world for the Lord. I love you.

–Mom and Dad: From the first moment I was placed in your care, you have loved me unconditionally and completely. You have both exampled uninhibited devotion to family and I admire and respect both of you more than words could adequately describe. Thank you for being the ones that rescued me as a baby, then nurtured me through the turbulence of my adolescence, and loved me through the other difficult events of my life. I love you very much and thank God for his sovereign plan in bringing us together.

–Bob and Phyllis: As your daughter–in–law, I couldn't be more blessed. Your love and generosity have impacted our family in incredible ways. You both have loved deeply and blessed me greatly. Who knew that night (Bob was trying to decide whether or not to go on our blind date), that our lives would be joined and result in blessings beyond what we could have possibly imagined. Thank you for encouraging him out the door that changed our lives forever. I love you.

-My faithful and most treasured friends (Pam, Katherine, Susan, Marlene, and Carol): Thank you all for your encouragement, faithfulness, and perseverance in helping me reach for my dreams. Your willingness to listen, provide feedback, and hold me accountable will triumphantly echo within my heart for eternity. Marlene, I wish I had a dollar for every time you said, "When are you going to quit your job and write your book?" I would be a rich woman. The light in your eyes and the confirmation through your words the first time I read my story aloud will be one of my fondest memories of our time together. In your face I saw an exhilaration that can only be shared by the bond we share as sisters in Christ. Pam, through geographical distance we have encouraged each other for over a quarter century. Each time we reunite that distance vanishes and we pick up where we left off. Thank you for being there for me. Katherine, you and I have a special bond that transcends boundaries and has encouraged me to be all that God created me to be. You are my accountability sister in Christ. Susan, you have been a treasured friend for many years. I don't think I have laughed harder or more often with any other friend. I thank you for your encouragement and support. As my sister, Carol, I appreciate the ongoing conversation and humor we share through the technology of texting. The "blip" is always a welcomed sound and the sharing that follows is usually uninhibited and soul baring. I love you dearly.

-Bible Study Fellowship (Beth, Jeanne, Ann, Rhonda, and Jackie): Beth, during the fall of 1992, you invited me to my first B.S.F. class. I attended the program for a total of nine years. Today, I can honestly proclaim that the program of study notes, lectures, group discussions, and fellowship gatherings transformed my faith and impacted my spiritual growth more than any other source of Biblical wisdom. Jeanne, Ann, and Rhonda's lectures are still influencing me today. The three of you became the voice of God in my head and I thank you from the bottom of my heart that the Lord blessed you with spiritual wisdom that taught me the love language of scripture. Jackie, you were my favorite discussion leader and I appreciated your insights the year we spent studying the life of Moses. Your humor and wit blessed me and I will always remember you fondly. Thank you all for your mentoring and friendship.

-Harvest Bible Chapel (James, Trent, Doug, and Micah): The teaching ministry of Harvest Bible Chapel is the place my husband and I call home. James; my husband, children, and I have listened to your radio ministry for many years and have benefitted from your tirelessness in study and exhortation. Trent, our pastor and friend; my husband, daughters, and I have been convicted through your impactful preaching since our first Sunday in the fall of 2011. Thank you for your passion and discipline in proclaiming biblical truth and its application to daily life. Doug, our children have been involved in your HBC in Indianapolis and we have been blessed to have you preside over the weddings of our daughters. We pray for your wisdom and discernment from afar, and are very thankful that you are their pastor. Micah, the passion and presence that you bring to worship touches my heart every worship service. You are uniquely gifted musically and I am moved spiritually each Sunday when you honor and worship the Lord through song.

-Crossbooks: My closing expressions of appreciation are for the staff of my publishing company, Crossbooks. From my first contact with your ministry, I have encountered one professional after another. I have received courtesy, honesty, and solid direction through all of the steps towards the publication of my book. I have never had a formal computer class and your willingness to instruct (with a little help from my daughters) and mentor me compassionately has been appreciated. Thank you for your guidance through my goal of publishing, *Moses and Me*.

CPSIA information can be obtained at www.ICGtesting.com
Printed in the USA
LVOW08s2303070913

351356LV00001B/32/P